A sacred space to meet with God

Enthusiasm

Welcome to *Airlock*!

Airlock is a Bible reading guide that contains 13 weeks' worth of undated material. You can use it whenever you like, wherever you like. There are six pages per week – five daily notes and a little extra for the weekend – but feel free to use it in the way that benefits you the most.

Each daily page is divided into three sections:

Decompress

This is a short prayer or thought designed to get you in the right frame of mind to read the Bible, and to prepare you for what you're about to read. After the Decompress section, you'll be given the Bible passage for the day. It doesn't matter what Bible version you use – just make sure you open up your Bible!

Immerse

This section contains ways of relating the Bible passage to today's culture. It also explains anything difficult in the Bible passage, and will help you understand the context the passage was written in.

Re-engage

This section encourages you to take what you've learned from the Bible passage and apply it to your day-to-day life through practical suggestions and pointers.

Contents

Airlock goes systematically through various books of the Bible. This is the fourth book in the series, although you don't have to read the books in order.

This issue we look at the power of prayer, **pay** Jonah **a visit and continue our voyage through the books of** Psalms, Isaiah, Matthew, Acts **and** 1 Corinthians.

Step into the *Airlock* and relieve the pressure!

Written by Jenny Baker (E/01–05), Dave Gatward (E/16–20), Lizzie Green (E/60–65), Howard Ingham (E/31–35), Nick Lear (E/21–25), James Lovelock (E/26–30), Ruth McCaughren (E/41–45), Anne Phipps (E/56–60), Al Rodgers (E/06–10, E/46–50), Alex Taylor (E/53), Steve Tilley (E/11–15, E/51–52, E/54–55) and Rachel Wild (E/36–40).

Designed and illustrated by Martin Lore. Cover photography by Chris Brown.

Cape fear

Decompress

Are you into scary theme park rides? It's fantastic to scream your head off while you grip the safety rail until your knuckles turn white. But deep down you know that really you're safe – they wouldn't let you on the ride if they thought you were in any danger.

NOW READ MATTHEW 14:22–36

Immerse

Richard Rodriguez is a US teacher whose hobby is setting world records on rollercoasters. Last summer he spent ten hours a day for three months on the 'mega coaster' Expedition GeForce in Germany. After all that time, scary must be the last word he'd use to describe the ride – maybe boring would be more appropriate, or even 'home'.

>Peter wasn't afraid of the storm at first – after all, he was a fisherman. He must have been out at night in bad weather hundreds of times in his life. But he was afraid of this strange figure walking across the water to him, until he realised it was Jesus. Then he wanted to do what Jesus was doing – to experience the thrill of walking on water. And he was fine, until he started to look at the wind and waves. Out of the comfort zone of his boat, he was faced with the potential danger he was in, and his courage failed.

>Peter didn't need to be afraid – because Jesus was there – but he did need to have faith. Hearing Jesus tell him to step out of the boat didn't mean that walking on water was suddenly easy. He needed to keep his eyes on Jesus, not on the circumstances he was in. And that was hard.

Re-engage

What is your comfort zone – what areas of life do you feel most comfortable in? How might Jesus be calling you to step out and do something different? Remember, adventure without risk is Disneyland. Take a moment to pray to God about these things.

Airlock: Enthusiasm

Themes: **Hypocrisy, Speech**

Right from the heart

Decompress

What words have come out of your mouth in the last 24 hours?

NOW READ MATTHEW 15:1-20

Immerse

The Pharisees were a religious and political party in New Testament times. They were very committed to keeping God's law as it was interpreted and applied by the scribes. The scribes started with the laws as written down in the Old Testament and then added their own beliefs about how these laws should be kept. These traditions and customs weren't written down but were passed on by word of mouth, and there were loads of them for the Pharisees to worry about.

>The Pharisees were hung up on rules and nit-picking. They seriously thought that it was a sin not to wash your hands before you ate. They made sure that everything they did followed some law or other so on the outside they were perfect people – or as near as they could get.

>Jesus looks deeper and says it's what's in your heart that's important; it's what comes out of you, in terms of thoughts, words and actions that reveals what you are really like inside.

Re-engage

Think back over what you have said about others in the last 24 hours. Pick two or three things that you wish you hadn't said. What was at the heart of those comments? Talk to God about them and ask for forgiveness. Do you need to do anything to put things right?

>Christians often get accused of hypocrisy. Why do you think other people expect us to be perfect?

>Jesus said, 'It is not what people put into their mouths that makes them unclean. It is what comes out of their mouths that makes them unclean.' Does this mean that words are more important than actions?

Airlock: Enthusiasm

Themes: **Inclusion, Prejudice**

Who let the dogs out?!

Decompress

Out of all the people that you know, who is the least likely to turn up at your church?

NOW READ MATTHEW 15:21–28

Immerse

It's generally accepted that it's a good thing to be inclusive – that everyone should have equal opportunities and people shouldn't be discriminated against because of their gender, ethnic group, disability and so on. But sometimes the desire to be inclusive can go a bit far. The headteacher of an infant school in West Yorkshire banned the story of The Three Little Pigs for fear of upsetting Muslim pupils. All other books featuring pigs, including *Babe*, were also put away. Muslims don't eat pork, but Islamic leaders say banning the books is ridiculous and they would never have recommended it.

Re-engage

The disciples couldn't imagine Jesus wanting to bother with this woman. But he did. She showed that she recognised him as the Messiah, and that she expected something from him, even if it was only the 'crumbs' of his attention that the Israelites didn't want. And Jesus couldn't resist responding to her faith – her daughter was healed. Are there people, or groups of people, who you or your church don't bother with?

>Jesus never turned anyone away from his kingdom – but often people excluded themselves because they didn't have enough faith, or weren't prepared to make sacrifices. Think back to the person who you identified as least likely to come to your church – and start praying for them to have an encounter with Jesus.

Airlock: Enthusiasm

Themes: **Miracles, Motivation**

Miracles on a mountainside

Decompress

'Lord, help us to see what you want to do in the lives of the people around us.'

NOW READ MATTHEW 15:29–39

Immerse

In the film *Bruce Almighty*, Jim Carrey plays Bruce, a frustrated TV reporter who meets God and is given all God's power for a week. As you might expect, he uses this power for his own benefit – from making his dog use the toilet instead of having 'accidents' in his flat and moving the moon to help him seduce his girlfriend, to making his rival at work make a complete mess of his TV news report. And, although he benefits, some of those actions have a terrible effect on other people. What would you have done differently if you had the same opportunity as him?

>Why do people lead worship, or pray for others, or stand up at the front and preach? I've done all those things and, to be honest, it can be hard to have completely pure motives sometimes. Yes, you want to see God at work, but it's also nice to have a pat on the back at the end, or to be told you've helped someone, or to be known as someone whose prayers get answered. But how mad is that? If God doesn't show up, then all of those things are useless anyway. As ever, we need to look to Jesus to see the right motivation in action. Jesus uses his power, not to gain popularity or fame, but to glorify God and to demonstrate his compassion for people.

Re-engage

You may not be able to pray and see God miraculously multiply your packed lunch, but you can try to have the same motivation as Jesus by seeking to glorify God and to act out of compassion in your everyday life. Think of someone in your family or among your friends who needs help. What secret act of service could you do for them that would show them someone has noticed what they need? Once you've thought of something, do it.

Airlock: Enthusiasm

Themes: **Discernment, Miracles**

Red sky at night...

Decompress

If you put a block of ice in the sun, it melts and turns to water.
>If you put a lump of clay in the sun, it dries out until it is rock hard. The same source of heat and light has the opposite effect on two different substances.

NOW READ MATTHEW 16:1-4

Immerse

Does this mean you should never ask God to give you a sign, or answer a prayer? The difference is in the reason for asking - the Pharisees and Sadducees were out to trick him. If Jesus had performed a miracle, whatever it was they would have found fault, or a reason to criticise him. They didn't really want to see a sign; they wanted Jesus to make a mistake they could pounce on. But he was too wise for that.

Re-engage

Think of a question that a non-Christian friend has asked you about God - like why does God allow suffering? Talk to your Christian friends about how they answer that question and think about your own point of view. Be ready for the next time that question comes up - not to parrot off an answer without thinking, but to show that you have really thought it through.
>The Pharisees and Sadducees had no excuse for not seeing who Jesus really was and what God was really like. Romans 1:18-20 says that God has shown us all there is to know about him through creation. If you look at the wonder of the world around you, you can see the fingerprints of God all over creation - but only if you want to see them. Remember the comment about the ice and the clay?

Airlock: Enthusiasm

If you were God for a week,
what miracles would you perform?

What would your motivation be?
To help others? To gain fame and
fortune? To attract members of the
opposite sex?

How difficult is it to stay true to what
God wants rather than what looks
good to the people around you?

Extra 1 Mark 13:38-40
Extra 2 Luke 7:36-50
Extra 3 Luke 11:37-54

Themes: **God's power, Universe**

Awesome

Decompress

If you had to come up with ten words to describe what God is like, what would they be? Do it now.

NOW READ PSALM 29

Immerse

Recently, I stood at the top of the Grand Canyon and looked down, and it's a long, long way to the bottom (a mile – just stop and think about it… a MILE… so far, it takes a day to walk down, and a day to walk back up!). I don't often run out of words, and sunsets, mountains, valleys and waterfalls don't really flick that 'awe' switch in me. But the Grand Canyon did. And that's kind of where Psalm 29 is coming from. Not just awe at stuff around, but awe at God, who's bigger than all that.

>Thunder, the ocean, lightning and floods probably don't sound that impressive to us. Not unless you stand right under a lightning strike, or you've had your house or village washed away by a flood. Then we'd start to remember just how powerful some of the things in the world around us are. These are probably the most powerful things in the world that David knew, and he picked them to compare with God, saying God is bigger and more powerful than all of them.

Re-engage

It's easy sometimes to only think about what God's done for us – or if it feels like he's not done what we wanted or expected, to think we haven't got much to thank him for. But Psalm 29 isn't about what God's done for anyone. It's just about how massive he is, and how he deserves our respect, just because… because he's there, and he is who he is.

>And in a 'consumer world' where most people, most of the time, do stuff because they think they can get something out of it, that's not normal. And it might make us stop and think. How much do we thank God when he's done something good for us? How much do we thank him on the boring or rubbish days – just because he's good?

>Psalm 29 is just about thanking God for who he is… so thank him. If it helps, go somewhere you find awe-inspiring, and then like the psalm, remember that God is bigger and better and more amazing than even that.

Airlock: Enthusiasm

Survive an assassination

Themes: **Hard times**

Decompress

If you think back over your life and had to draw a graph of the highs and lows, what would it look like? What would the highs be? Where would the lows be?

NOW READ PSALM 30

Immerse

I've never nearly died. I've never had people trying to kill me. I've never had to beg God to save my life. (Maybe I'm not living life dangerously enough!)

>But I have had nightmare situations where God has turned up and turned them around. I have had times when I should have been stressed, but God kept me focused and chilled. I have had sad times that God came into and brought hope, and even happiness (but not dancing… I don't do dancing). I have had times when I was scared, but God stood with me, and I felt safe again.

>Our lives might be different from David's, but it's the same God we're talking to.

Re-engage

If Psalm 29 is about how God deserves our respect just because of who he is, Psalm 30 is about respect for God because he got involved in our lives.

>Of course this is all locked into the life of one guy, which might be completely different from the ways God has changed our lives, but it does show that God didn't just make this amazing world and then go to find his pipe and slippers and spend the rest of eternity stroking a cat in a rocking chair, doing the *Times* crossword (and giving Werthers Originals to small boys). He stuck around to get involved in our lives now – our complicated and messy lives.

>This psalm is full of contrasts in David's life, showing how much difference God can make. Take a couple of minutes to look back through the psalm, and see what those contrasts are. Think about your life. Would there be many before God/after God contrasts? Anything you want to thank him for?

Airlock: Enthusiasm

Bad day

Themes: **Suffering**

Decompress

Have you ever thought you could do a better job than God?

NOW READ PSALM 31

Immerse

Do we ever feel like God's messed up, or do we ever slip into giving God tips on how to deal with stuff when we pray, or even blatantly tell him what to do?

>David was in a place that's got to be about as grim as it gets (being tracked by enemies, totally drained and knackered, hated, judged, frozen out by friends, forgotten, insulted, scared and death plots). And, no surprise, he's not jumping about yelling, 'Thanks God for getting me here, I want to stay here forever!' He's not crazy – he does want things to change, and he asks God to act (save me, protect me, lead me, guide me, have mercy, show your kindness, let the wicked be disgraced and lie silent in the grave, silence their lying lips), but he's not laying into God or telling God what to do.

>In fact, right there, mixed in with the list of nightmares and asking for help, is some amazing stuff about God ('Lord I trust you … for the good of your name … I give you my life … I will be glad and rejoice in your love … how great is your goodness…'). It's not like David's pretending that everything's OK, thinking that if he ignores the nightmares they will go away, or like he thinks yelling good stuff about God is some magic spell which will get rid of all the bad stuff. And he's not telling God how to run things better. It just looks like, even though everything was so bad, David still trusted that God was real, was there, still cared, and was somehow, sometime, going to change things. I'm not sure I'd have lasted as long as David did.

Re-engage

We probably all have some kind of micro (or not so micro) nightmare going on in our lives somewhere. Can you look at that situation and see how God is still good, even if, like for most of this psalm, the nightmare hasn't gone away? Psalm 31 does two things at the same time – it remembers what God is like (and thanks him) and it is honest about the nightmare (and asks God to get involved). Can you do both now?

Airlock: Enthusiasm

Themes: **Confession, Forgiveness**

Don't be a donkey

Decompress

Do you feel guilty about anything right now? Stuff which you can't think about without feeling bad? Get ready to meet with God – and let him deal with the guilt.

NOW READ PSALM 32

Immerse

The thing about insurance is, until you need it, you ignore it (and then when a drunk driver smashes into your parked car one Tuesday night, you hope you remembered to send off that cheque…)
>But in this Psalm, David remembers that you can't treat God like an insurance policy… you can't ignore him until disaster hits. God isn't just there for when things go wrong. If he's worth knowing in the rough times, he's worth knowing in the good times, too (and it will make us more ready for the rough times when they come). But David didn't always remember that…
>In verses 3 and 4, David shows us what happens when we mess up and try to deal with it without God. He knew he'd messed up, but instead of coming to God and saying sorry, he spirals into unfocused self-pity. All that changes when he chucks away self-pity and turns it into real, totally honest, focused confession – 'fessing up to God all the stuff that went wrong. God swapped self-pity for forgiveness, chucked away the guilt, mixed in some new protection, and showed him the right way ahead.

Re-engage

So, like the man says in the Psalm, don't treat God like an insurance policy that only kicks in when things go really wrong. 'Don't be a … donkey' (verse 9). Pray to God now before things go so wrong you can't remember how to (verse 6). And be free (verses 1 and 2).
>Sometimes guilt is something we just need to sort out between God and us. Other times things that have gone wrong don't just get in the way between God and us. They get in the way between us and other people. Do you need to go and ask to be forgiven by anyone?

Airlock: Enthusiasm

Themes: **Freedom**

The Matrix Rewritten?

Decompress

Since Psalm 29, we've been through giving respect to God because of who he is, thanking God for what he's done for us, total despair and saying sorry. Where are you with God today?

NOW READ PSALM 33

Immerse

Chances are you've seen *The Matrix*. It's one of those films that everybody's got an angle on. Christians, Buddhists, film techies, martial arts guys… and probably a whole load more has been read into the film than the makers ever meant to be there.

>But, looking at *The Matrix* (no, we've not forgotten it's fiction), and then at something like this psalm, you start to see how much freedom God has given us.

>After a bit about music at the start (verses 1 and 2), this psalm (or song) digs right in with what God is like (true, fair, right, loves the world – verses 4 and 5), what he did (made the world – verses 6-9), and what he does now (is in control, knows and understands us – verses 10-15). Then it looks at our options – to try and stick it out on our own (verses 16,17), or work with God and trust him (verses 18-20).

Re-engage

It's a million miles from a Matrix-like world which has an 'Architect', hidden away behind a whole world which isn't much more than a computer-generated mirage controlling the characters trapped in it, and a small army of rebels (or heroes) fighting to reach a way of being free from the Matrix. With God, we don't get freedom by running away from him (or fighting our way free in the world's longest martial arts scenes – is it just me that heads towards sleep in those bits?). We find freedom by going back to him and finding his plan for us and our world. A good reason to thank him… just like the psalm does.

>'We rejoice in him, because we trust his holy name. Lord, show your love to us as we put our hope in you.' (verses 21,22)

Airlock: Enthusiasm

1. Sing to the Lord, you who do what is right;
   honest people should praise him.
2. Praise the Lord on the harp;
   make music for him on a ten-stringed lyre.
3. Sing a new song to him;
   play well and joyfully.

Try writing a new psalm – telling God how you feel. Even if you're not musical (you don't have to sing it!), or a great writer (God is more interested in you being honest than how many prizes it would win).

Handwritten annotations:

Oh Lord, you are great really great
Most worthy nice to me
almighty
omnipotent
very big absolutely fantastic

I will praise you in the highest
tabernacle
my front room

Worthy are you to be exalted
I think you're cool

make music for him on a
ten stringed lyre
make music on the decks?
a Gibson Les Paul?

Though I walk through the valley
of the shadow of death
yet will I fear no evil.
Even when things are tough
you're there.

This psalm starts off with music. Why do you think worshipping God and music are so close together in the Bible, and in most churches now? Can music ever get in the way? Are there other ways you find it easier to worship God?

Other good songs...
Extra 1 Exodus 15
Extra 2 Luke 1:46–55

Themes: **Spiritual gifts, Maturity**

Tongue-tied

Decompress

We all act out of mixed motives from time to time, don't we? It seems as if some people in the Corinthian church (who could speak in tongues) did it to show off rather than help others. Enter Paul and his bottomless bag of pastoral advice.

NOW READ 1 CORINTHIANS 14:6–21

Immerse

You are in another country where the language is unfamiliar and you want to buy some food at the market. Can you cope? Well, yes. First, you point to what you want and indicate with signs whether the portion being measured out is too much or too little. Then (here's the tough bit), you trust the stallholder to take the right amount of money out of your hand. You need to risk being misunderstood and trust the other person's honesty. As you depart, the stallholder thanks you clearly in your own language. Durr. She understood all along.

>Paul's Corinthian church seems to have had lots of people having a go at communicating using strange languages, with God and with each other, but they had forgotten that they all had the ability to speak plainly. And Paul loves plain-speaking churches growing in their faith.

>Speaking in tongues. What's that then? Simply put, it's expressing words of praise, prayer or prophecy in another, unfamiliar language. It is a gift God has given for building up the church. But it will only build the church up if it is explained. Thus Paul's comments that tongues should be interpreted (verse 13) and that words people can understand are more important (verse 19).

Re-engage

1 Corinthians 12:31 says that we should 'truly want to have the greater gifts.' Don't get too sidetracked by the gift of tongues which, whilst important to some, is a lesser gift.

>If you have no experience of people speaking in tongues, and you are interested, ask around amongst your friends or in your church to see if there is someone who can help you understand it.

Airlock: Enthusiasm

Themes: **Spiritual gifts, Evangelism**

Who told you that?

Decompress

You walk into a room full of strangers. Not only are they talking about you (always a worry) but they know things that you haven't ever told anyone. Interested? Gonna stay? You betcha.

NOW READ 1 CORINTHIANS 14:22–25

Immerse

Think about the last time you walked into a place that was unfamiliar to you. It may have been a hospital, a busy office or maybe even a theatre or stadium. When everyone else looks as if they know what they are doing and where they are going, you can feel awfully lonely, even in a crowd.

>As ever, Paul is anxious for the health of non-Christians. He never lets his readers forget what it must be like to be a stranger in church. He wants people to feel welcome and even challenged. The worst thing for Paul would be for a newcomer to leave because they were confused about what was going on. I've got to agree.

>Paul seems, at first, to have slightly confusing advice for his readers. On the one hand, he encourages clarity in meetings (verse 19); on the other he says that speaking in different languages (tongues) will be a proof for those who do not believe (verse 22). Then he says if you all speak in tongues outsiders will think you are mad (verse 23). Let's unscramble it:

>1 It is good to teach clearly.
>2 Tongues can help others believe in God.
>3 If everyone 'babbles' in a strange language, outsiders will have no way of distinguishing Christianity from any other faith/cult where people do mad things and into which one has to be initiated.

>So speak clearly and sometimes use tongues; but don't all use tongues at once. Easy. Finally, prophecy (speaking out words of truth revealed by God) will be a powerful evangelistic tool.

Re-engage

How much of what your church does would seem mad to outsiders? Is it different in your youth group or home group, or is that equally as strange? Start a conversation and think about changing them.

>Go somewhere unfamiliar. Note the things that made you feel welcome and those which excluded you. Feed these feelings and thoughts into your discussion about your church.

Airlock: Enthusiasm

Order, order

Themes: **Spiritual gifts, Peace**

Decompress

Would you go to a club if they always played the same tunes in the same order? It might be a nice comforting old friend of a place to return to from time to time; you'd always know where you were and what to expect. But every week? Probably not.

NOW READ 1 CORINTHIANS 14:26–40

Immerse

A student I know ran out of money a week before the end of term. All that was left in the food cupboard was a large bag of rice and some soy sauce. So that was what he lived on for a week. When he got home, his parents asked him what he wanted to eat. Anything he said, except rice and soy sauce. Variety is an essential part of life, not just in a balanced food diet but in a spiritual diet too.

>The content of the church meetings at Corinth sounds a bit 'interesting'. Everyone who liked prophecy prophesied; those who liked singing got on with songs. Others spoke in tongues while still others taught each other. To an outsider it must have felt like listening to five or six people talking at the same time – all interesting but not understandable. Order was needed.

>The instruction to women to remain silent seems particularly bound up with a 2,000-year-old culture. We need to take the broad principle, that worship should be structured without necessarily insisting on there being tongues, prophets and silent women at every service.

Re-engage

Whatever gifts you use, remember they must be used with self-control. The Corinthian church seems to have lost track of this. What side of the line is your church on – wildly different or boringly repetitive? Or has it got it just right?

>Could you and your friends devise an act of worship for others to take part in? How about organising a service at your local church if you can?

Airlock: Enthusiasm

Theme: **Resurrection**

Believe it or not

Decompress

The most gob-smacking, mind-blowing, stomach-churning, life-improving news of all time. Expose your verrucas, brothers and sisters; this passage makes burning bushes passé.

NOW READ 1 CORINTHIANS 15:1–11

Immerse

How many witnesses do you need to convince you? As I write, a film crew is at work less than 100 metres away from my home. Really. There is a small area of public open space just near my house which is quite a popular TV location. I keep popping along to nose about and see if anyone famous is there. It's true. It is. You could ask other members of my family, my neighbours or all the members of the Leamington Spa dog-walking fraternity. You don't have to take my word for it. The crowd of witnesses builds up and eventually the sheer weight of numbers convinces you. All those people can't be telling porkies, surely?

>See what I did there? Same argument as Paul in our passage. If you don't believe him you could ask: Peter/The 12 Apostles/The 500 disciples (OK, some have died but only a few)/James

>Jesus is alive and these people (all of them) will tell you about it.

Re-engage

There's only one thing to preach really, one question to ask – do you believe Jesus is alive?

>Why not ask a few people that question this week, when they are least expecting it.

>Do you believe Jesus is alive?

Airlock: Enthusiasm

Theme: **Resurrection**

Useless

Decompress

If everything you do in your whole life is based on one premise, what happens if it crumbles? This is foundational stuff. If we are wrong our whole life and faith collapses. Bit embarrassing really.

NOW READ 1 CORINTHIANS 15:12–34

Immerse

Ever seen a ceremony where a local, or indeed national dignitary, cements in a foundation stone. Work is about to begin on some new famous building and this stone will be crucial. It is often the corner stone and will bear the weight of two huge walls. If anything happens to the foundation stone, the whole structure will collapse. That is why it is usually big and different to the ordinary building bricks being used.

>My knowledge of bricks just ran out. But I do know that Jesus' resurrection from the dead is the foundation stone in my own faith. If I ever start to doubt that, then my whole life will be in danger of collapse.

>Verse 12 tells us why this whole section (from the beginning of chapter 15) has been written. Some Corinthians had written to Paul about the resurrection of the dead. The thrust of the passage is not to prove that Jesus is alive, but to argue from that fact to the resurrection of all believers.

>Paul puts it this strongly. If no one is raised then Christ has not been raised; the two are completely interlinked. Furthermore, if Christ has not been raised our preaching is useless.

Re-engage

'Come back to your right way of thinking...' (verse 34). Nuff said.

>Look at a wall. Notice the way it is built. You could remove a brick and the whole thing would remain standing. But remove a foundation stone? Well, take a wild guess.

Airlock: Enthusiasm

In our churches, we can get so hung up on what we do and the way we do it. In chapter 14 of 1 Corinthians, Paul gives us some simple rules to live by. But then in chapter 15, he reminds us what it is all about – Christ.

Christ died for our sins,
as the Scriptures say.
He was buried,
and three days later
he was raised to life,
as the Scriptures say.
1 Corinthians 15:3a,4

What is your church like? Is there anything you want to change? Is there anyone you can talk to constructively about it? Is there anything in your life (a 'law' or tradition) which is getting in the way of remembering what you believe in and telling someone about Christ? Or do you need to be reminded of why you believe?

Extra 1 Philippians 2:6–11
Extra 2 Colossians 1:15–23

Themes: **Time for God, Prayer**

Time alone

Decompress

Before you do anything, sit down, close your eyes and clear your mind. This is you and God time. Sometimes it's easy to pray while you're doing other things, but this is special time where nothing else is going on. So make that clear to yourself and to the Creator you're in the presence of.

NOW READ MATTHEW 6:5-8

Immerse

Life is full of huge distractions. And it's getting more like that every day. As soon as you wake up in the morning, the pressure is on to do things, to make an impression, to stay busy, to be something. And it can be easy to base our lives on the things we do, what we wear, what we're interested in, rather than who we are and what we're really about. We forget to spend time alone, and when we do, we fill that time with the telly, computer games, music, magazines, DVDs. These distractions get in the way of us finding out about ourselves.

>And before we know it, we're nothing more than a shallow puddle of reflections of what the world is about, rather than a deep ocean of individual ideas that are God-inspired. And to learn about ourselves, who we really are and what we're really about, we need to spend time alone, away from any outside influences, in the presence of God.

Re-engage

All it takes is a few minutes each day. Set a time and a place. Each day, go to that place at that time and spend just ten minutes in the presence of God. If you want, take along a Bible to read. And why not take a note book – sometimes it's helpful to write your prayers to God. It helps you focus on what you're talking and thinking about and stops your brain wandering off and thinking about what's on at the cinema.

>Create a space – in your own room create an area that's for you and God. Clear it of distractions and replace them with things that'll help you get with your creator. Think about what's used in church to help people do this – pictures, candles, the Bible, meditative music. Add to this space over the following months and before you know it you'll have your own little worship area.

Airlock: Enthusiasm

Themes: **Priorities, Giving**

The Lord's prayer

Decompress

Think about what's important to you in your life. Now think again – just how important are the things you're thinking of? Could you survive without them? Ask God to help you focus on the things in your life which he knows really matter.

NOW READ LUKE 11:1–4

Immerse

I read something a couple of days ago about adverts. It seems that those people who want us to buy their stuff are getting panicky. It seems that we, the public, don't watch their adverts anymore. We switch channels and pre-record. It seems we've had enough. What I'd like, though, is to see this go a bit further. For everyone to not just stop watching adverts, but also to stop going out and buying stuff. Wishful thinking, I guess, but it could be a quiet revolution.

>Take what Jesus says here through the Lord's prayer. It's a lesson in back-to-basics. We praise God first, we ask for that which we need to live; no more, no less, and then we deal with our own sin, forgiving others, and asking not to be put through something we'd never survive. So many of us seem to spend a lot of time wishing for more things that we don't really need, spending too much cash on trying to get them, and getting into debt. What's the point? We need to learn to appreciate what we've got and to stop getting so obsessed with what we haven't and what we don't really need.

Re-engage

We all need to appreciate the things we actually need in our lives and to forget the things we don't, to get it all in balance. You probably don't need new trainers or ten new CDs, but you'd be a bit lost without food and water. Appreciate the basics again, and praise the Lord for them.

>So you're saving up for something are you? Well, perhaps it's something you need, perhaps it isn't, but why not try this... You've got a set amount to save up, so why not save ten per cent more and give the cash to charity? New MP3 player costing you £100? That's only an extra £10 to find, and it'll be doing some good, too. And if you do this once, what's to stop you doing it for more stuff? Nothing

Airlock: Enthusiasm

Themes: **God the parent**

Daddy

Decompress

Think of your relationship with God. What's it actually like? Is it one full of trust, excitement, forgiveness, love and hope? Is it simply routine, going through the motions? Or does it have a mix of both? What kind of relationship do you want with God?

NOW READ ROMANS 8:14–17; GALATIANS 4:6,7

Immerse

If there's one thing teenagers are good at, it's hating their parents. It's as though there's something in the programming - parents are great up to the age of 12, but as soon as you turn 13, they're the enemy. Parents become control freaks, people out of touch, people who don't understand, people who never give you what you want when you want it.

>Get a bit older though, and if the parents have done their job correctly, things change. You start to look back and see that your parents were quite often right. They weren't doing things to spite you, or restricting you because it was fun. They were actually guiding you, helping you to grow, to learn, to become the best you could be - the you that you look at now in the mirror. OK, so there's a lot of work to do, but if people actually take time to look at the role their parents have had in the people they've become, they'll probably be pleasantly surprised.

>Can there really be any better analogy of what God is than our parent - both father and mother to us, guiding us, chastising us, helping us, having faith in us no matter what, and always willing to forgive?

Re-engage

If God's our ultimate parent, perhaps we should start being the son or daughter of God we know we can be. It takes time and effort, but that's no bad thing. Often by working hard, by pushing and challenging ourselves, we come to be so much more than we were.

>Write down all the qualities that you think make a great parent. Now think - what's stopping you having all those qualities yourself?

Airlock: Enthusiasm

Themes: **Hard times, Loneliness**

Desperation prayers

Decompress

You know what it's like when it seems as though everything's going wrong, that no one loves or understands you, that God is miles away or doesn't exist. But God's somewhere out there and maybe we need to scream and shout.

NOW READ PSALM 102

Immerse

OK, so this may not sound cool, but if you've got any sense of individuality in you, you'll go with me on this one. Get hold of a copy of *Jesus Christ Superstar*. I'm talking about the original film of the stage play. The one that's all flares. What I want you to do is listen to the track Gethsemane. This is where Jesus goes off alone to pray to God about the days ahead, knowing that he will be scorned, rejected, tortured, slaughtered.

>The reason the film's so good is because Ted Neeley, the bloke playing Jesus, screams so much passion into his part, that it gives you a whole new insight into what might have been going through Jesus' mind at the time. This was the one time when Jesus questioned everything – his life, his mission, his God. And in *Superstar*, we're introduced to the humanity of Jesus in such a way that it leaves you breathless. Sometimes we forget that Jesus was both God and man. He had his questions, his doubts. And he screams them at God. Just like we do. So, no matter what you're going through, Jesus does understand and you are not as alone as you think, even in the storms of life. And God is listening.

Re-engage

Sometimes, when life is really crashing down, we ignore God when we need him the most. Or, we try to pray but don't really know what to say or do. We shouldn't. Sometimes, just through the very passion of our confusion and desperation, we get through.

>So angry you want to scream? What's stopping you? Do one of two things – make a compilation CD of all your favourite screaming songs and use them to help you to focus. Or write. Yes, write. Get that pen out and craft your pain on to the paper. Scream and yell at God, get across exactly what you think.

>And if you think you're too angry and that your language might stray, understand this – God isn't someone you can shock. He understands you and, when everything gets too much, all we can do is just let it all go. God isn't going to turn away.

Airlock: Enthusiasm

Themes: **Prayer, God listens**

Answered prayer

Decompress

When things are bad, it's as though God never listens. But think about your life, the paths you've walked so far. Can you see God's guiding hand? Can you remember those times when your prayers have been answered so obviously that you just want to scream about it? Thank God for those moments now.

NOW READ PSALM 66

Immerse

Imagine you're someone who wants to be a full-time writer. And you don't want to just scrape by, you want your writing to be successful, read by millions across the world. People tell you you're mad. Have more sensible ideas, they say. You write something and send it to a publisher. It gets rejected. What do you do? Give up? Or look at it again, make it better? Or dump it and try something new? Well, you do both, and you send it off again. And again it gets rejected. And again you change your writing, learn more. And you send it off, and... so do you give up or keep trying? Imagine if you keep trying and nothing happens.

>Imagine you eventually get it right and you're getting published. Suddenly, after all that persistence, all that hard work, all the times you've wanted to give up and run away, it's worked. That's what it's like when your prayers are answered. Sometimes we're praying about the wrong stuff, asking for the wrong things. God knows this, gives us time to work it out and guides us, until we're going the right way, doing the right things, and everything clicks into place and our prayers are answered and God smiles with us.

Re-engage

If your prayers aren't getting answered (ie you're getting the answers you don't want), have a think about the things you're praying for. Does something not seem quite right? Are you expecting the answers to be a certain thing? Are you open minded enough to think about why the answers are something different? Perhaps you need to look at your prayers like a rejected manuscript – it's got potential, but needs work.

>Take something you're passionately praying about now. Write it down. Look at it. Try to work out what God thinks of it – and remember he can see the whole picture, not just your viewpoint. Time for a revision?

Airlock: Enthusiasm

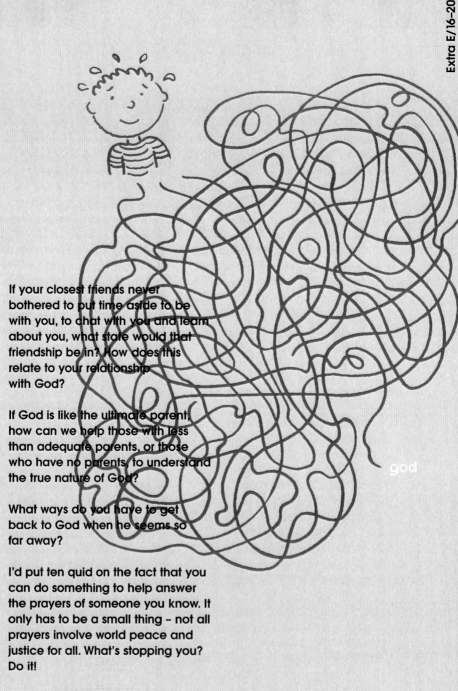

If your closest friends never bothered to put time aside to be with you, to chat with you and learn about you, what state would that friendship be in? How does this relate to your relationship with God?

If God is like the ultimate parent, how can we help those with less than adequate parents, or those who have no parents, to understand the true nature of God?

What ways do you have to get back to God when he seems so far away?

I'd put ten quid on the fact that you can do something to help answer the prayers of someone you know. It only has to be a small thing – not all prayers involve world peace and justice for all. What's stopping you? Do it!

Extra 1 Luke 18:1-14
Extra 2 John 17

Themes: **Criticism, Belief, Faith**

Bready, steady, cook

Decompress

What criticisms and negative attitudes do your friends, family or others have about your faith? How much attention do you pay them?

> Ask God to help you sift through these criticisms to see if any are valid and, if they are, to give you the wisdom to explore them and the grace to change.

NOW READ MATTHEW 16:5–12

Immerse

How often have you heard people laugh about you being a Christian? How many times have they told you that you can't believe in the Bible because it is full of contradictions? How often have people been surprised when you've told them you went to church recently? Have people asked you to prove that there is a God, or that your faith works?

> Don't feel under pressure from these people. They don't usually know what they're talking about and are repeating what they have heard other people say. Their motive is not to engage in a serious discussion about God, but either to change the subject or to discredit you because your faith makes them feel uncomfortable. Jesus warns us to beware of such attitudes because, just as yeast affects a whole batch of dough, these attitudes can affect the whole of society without having any basis in truth.

Re-engage

Jesus spoke about the yeast of the Pharisees and Sadducees, rather than their negativity, in order to get his disciples thinking. He did not spoon-feed them, but tried to stimulate them to think about their faith in the context of their life. We should never imagine that being a Christian means we do not have to think!

> 'Doubts are the ants in the pants of faith. They keep us alive and moving' (Frederich Beuchner). This is only true if they motivate us to explore our faith further. There is nothing wrong with having doubts or asking questions about faith. Think back to the last negative attitude or comment you received about your faith and try to come up with an answer. You may need to visit a local library or borrow some books from your youth leaders or vicar, but try to find out for yourself.

Airlock: Enthusiasm

Themes: **Understanding**

Eureka!

Decompress

My name means 'leader'; my wife's name means 'princess'. Do you know what your name means? If you don't know, look it up on the Internet and be prepared to be surprised. How appropriate is the meaning of your name?

NOW READ MATTHEW 16:13–20

Immerse

The Greek scientist Archimedes was trying to work out how you could measure the volume of objects while he was having a bath. He suddenly realised that the amount the water rose was an indicator of his volume and shouted, 'Eureka!' He was so excited he ran naked down the street! Jesus' reaction to Peter's expression of faith is similar: 'YES!!! At long last he understands.'

>All of us have those moments in our life. Moments when suddenly we understand more about who Jesus is and what his life means. It may be a sudden understanding of one of his parables or his teaching, or someone else might help us make sense of something about Jesus that was puzzling us, or it could be a bolt out of the blue.

Re-engage

How do you work out who Jesus is? Do you set aside a special time with him? (I guess so since that's what you are doing now.) Do you read his Word? Do you talk with him and with others about him?

>Even though you are to be commended for all these things, ultimately what you believe about Jesus is a gift from God. Paul writes that 'no one can say, "Jesus is Lord," without the help of the Holy Spirit' (1 Corinthians 12:3).

>Reread verse 17, inserting your name in place of 'Simon son of Jonah'. Hear Jesus tell you that you are blessed because God has revealed things to you about who Jesus is.

>Jesus reinforced his change of Simon's name to 'Rocky' (OK, 'Peter', but that's what it means) to show that God was going to use him as a foundation for his church. What names might he give you? Don't think of names like 'Vera' or 'Eric' but think of attributes that he wants to bring out in you such as 'Considerate' or 'Perceptive'. Ask him to tell you what names he would like to call you.

Airlock: Enthusiasm

Themes: **God's perspective, Trust**

Sublime to ridiculous

Decompress

Have you ever said something that made you feel really small or silly? A friend of mine wrote a science essay at school about micro-organisms, but missed out the 'ni'. The thoughtful teacher read it out to the whole class, to my friend's complete embarrassment.

>How would you feel if Jesus turned to you in public and said, 'Go away from me, Satan! You are not helping me!'

NOW READ MATTHEW 16:21–28; 20:17–19

Immerse

In the film *Terminator 2*, Arnie Schwarzenegger's cyborg character promises (with an Austrian accent), 'I'll be back!' just before he heads off to deal with those who are going to hurt the child he is programmed to protect. The Terminator did come back (after several million pounds worth of special effects).

>Jesus made a similar promise to his followers about his death and resurrection – he was coming back. There were no special effects; this was for real. If he could make and keep a promise that he would return from the dead, how reliable does that make him? The problem was that Peter did not believe him about the coming back bit. He was preoccupied with the dying bit that happened first.

Re-engage

Look at the reason Jesus gives for what he says to Peter: 'You don't care about the things of God, but only about the things people think are important.' What are your priorities? Do you want what God wants, or what you want? You only really know when there is a conflict between the two.

>In the 'Lord's prayer' (Matthew 6:9–13) Jesus encourages us to pray that God's will should be done. We need to pray for those things in our own lives as much as in the rest of the world. What are your priorities for the rest of the day? What do you want to do? What do you think God's priorities are? Pray through the Lord's prayer. Pray particularly that God's priorities will be your priorities: 'Your will be done.'

Airlock: Enthusiasm

Themes: **Who is Jesus?, Listening**

No doubt

Decompress

What's the best experience you have ever had? I mean the very best. The absolute number one. How long did the feeling of elation or exhilaration last? Didn't you feel at that moment that you wanted it to last for ever?

NOW READ MATTHEW 17:1–13

Immerse

Peter felt elated on top of the mountain with Jesus, Moses and Elijah, until he heard God's voice!

>Why is it significant that Jesus was talking with Moses and Elijah? Look back at 16:14 – some people were saying that Jesus was Elijah. This is because the Bible says that Elijah would return just before the Messiah came (Malachi 4:5). Jesus described John the Baptist as being the Elijah figure for him (Matthew 11:14).

>This passage is about establishing who Jesus really is. We have already heard that from Peter's lips (Matthew 16:16), and this passage is rich with evidence of Jesus' true identity. One of the pieces of evidence is that Elijah really had come back. (Add Jesus' physical transformation, and God's voice saying that he is his Son, and you get a pretty convincing case.)

Re-engage

God spoke some awesome words about Jesus. We heard some of them at his baptism: Jesus was God's Son, whom he loved, and he was very pleased with him (Matthew 3:17). But now there are some new words. They form the basis for God's advice about life: 'Listen to him!'

>If Jesus really is God's Son, we can surely find no better source of ideas and inspiration about life than him. If he is who he seems to be, then following his teaching has to be the best philosophy in life – or do you know someone more reliable, with better credentials to tell you about life?

>What do you find the most inspiring thing that Jesus said? Is it a parable, some teaching, a conversation he had with someone? Write it somewhere where you will be reminded of it during the next 24 hours.

>What do Jesus' words mean in your life? If it means making some changes, make them. If it means saying sorry to someone, do it now (by text, email, phone or in person). If it means doing something you find difficult, promise him you'll try (he promises he'll help you if you try).

>'Listen to him!'

Airlock: Enthusiasm

Themes: **Faith**

Mountain movers?

Decompress

What are the things in your life that loom large like mountains? What things seem impossible or really difficult at the moment? Be honest with God right now and tell him how tough these things are for you.

NOW READ MATTHEW 17:14-23

Immerse

On the face of it, Jesus seems to be saying that if only we have enough faith, we can move mountains. If this is so, then obviously the reason the mountains in our lives don't move is that we don't have enough faith. STOP! Don't beat yourself up with this lie.

>The issue here is not his disciples' lack of faith (otherwise he would not have said that they only needed faith as microscopic as a tiny mustard seed). The issue is the quality, not quantity of their faith. It would seem that Jesus' followers had been trying to force out the demons based on their own self-confidence and experience, not relying on God, which explains his exasperation with them in verse 17. When would they ever learn?

Re-engage

So what about those mountains? They still aren't moving. The issue is what the mountains represent. Moving mountains was a way of describing overcoming great difficulties (Isaiah 40:4) for God's people as a nation, not individuals. Here Jesus is talking about overcoming opposition to his kingdom, not about personal problems. If you want more proof, look at the number of times in the preceding passages (and this one) where Jesus has been talking about his death and resurrection.

>So what are those problems and issues you thought of earlier? Have faith in Christ that he can help you. He never promised anyone that they would not face problems, but he did promise that he would be with us by his Spirit, and that we would never have to endure more than we can bear with him (1 Corinthians 10:13).

>Ask Jesus to help you see that there is something on the other side of the mountain. Ask him to resolve the problem (after all, he healed the man's son in the story). But we also need to remember that he taught us to pray 'Your will be done', too. Ask him to help you to cope with life as it is at present, and ask him to show you someone you can talk with and pray with about these big issues. Give them a call, email or text now while you think about it.

Airlock: Enthusiasm

Who do you think Jesus is?
Don't just answer that with the usual
words that you use in church,
but think about it for a moment.
Write it down.

What are the implications for you of
what you have written? If what you
have written really does describe
Jesus, then what does that say
about your friendship with him?

What is the best description of Jesus
that you have ever heard?

Extra 1_ John 1:1-34
Extra 2_ Revelation 1:9-20

Themes: **God's plan, Justice**

The Next Generation

Decompress

This week's passages show how God kept the promise made to Jacob after he had stolen his brother Esau's birthright and was forced to flee the country. Recap that promise by reading Genesis 28:13–15.

NOW READ GENESIS 29:15-30

Immerse

God's plan to save the Jews (and later the world) happened over thousands of years and involved a huge cast of heroes and villains, and a massive amount of extras. And here we are at episode three of God's epic Redemption Plan…

>But there are always obstacles to disrupt God's plans - and this time the villain of the piece is Uncle Laban, who has already made a cameo appearance in Isaac: Quest for a woman. And if you thought he was a snide, greedy, snively little worm in that film, you ain't seen nothing yet.
I expect Jacob couldn't believe his luck when he met Rachel straight after having such a lovely conversation with God. 'Phwoar! My luck's in!' Could a fairytale ending really be so easy to find?

>The answer was 'no' then, and remains 'no' now. I had my 'Jacob's ladder' experience with God at the age of 15, with just as many skeletons in my closet as Jacob. And, although the effects of my meeting with God lasted for a couple of months, things didn't suddenly become wonderful with lovely skippy bunnies and, 'Ooh, look I've won the lottery'.

>God wanted Jacob to be part of his plan, but he needed Jacob to be more refined (and not in the sense of 'Good gracious, Mr Darcy, you're making me blush') and to understand what God wanted of him. In the same way, God wants you to be part of his ongoing plan (see Matthew 28) - but struggles and obstacles are going to be inevitable. There are a lot of Labans about…

Re-engage

It's sometimes worth looking over your journey so far to try to understand where you are now. Today, look back at when you became a Christian. Did it happen over time, or was there one particular moment when you can say you met with God? What promises did God make? Has he kept them all? Have a bit of a reminisce with God to help remind you how you became involved in his plan…

Airlock: Enthusiasm

Themes: **Family, God's plan**

Family dysfunctions

Decompress

'When I felt safe, I said, "I will never fear." Lord, in your kindness you made my mountain safe. But when you turned away, I was frightened' (Psalm 30:6,7).

NOW READ GENESIS 29:31 – 30:24

Immerse

Well, it's the classic romantic movie plot. It's got everything – love at first sight, a thwarted romance, the hero sacrificing himself for his beloved, bigamy. Yes, sir, when you get that old 'bridegroom marries the bride's sister by accident and then marries her as well' storyline, then you know there will not be a snot-free hanky in the cinema. But it's not a happy ending and, in fact, the whole unsavoury episode is treated a little bit like a football match by Jacob's two wives.

>'Well, it's half-time here in the bedroom, and Leah has made all the running with four early goals, while Rachel seems to be struggling to get going. She's tried all sorts of formations, but to no avail. Then she brought on a substitute – that's a third wife for Jacob. Two goals from penalties for the substitute Bilhah, but then Leah also brought on her substitute, Zilpah, who fired a shot into the back of the net.'

>The whole thing ends up an utter mess – we're up to Rachel 2, Leah 6 (plus two away goals for Leah's slave Zilpah) – and both Rachel's goals are from penalties… It seems way out of control. But God has a plan to use Jacob's devotion to his second wife, and finally allows Rachel to conceive a son who would remind Jacob of her. Altogether now – 'Give me my coloured coat…'

Re-engage

Can you imagine God's reactions to these goings on? And yet, despite the depravity and misguided selfishness of Jacob, Rachel and Leah, God still managed to work his plan out. He created the twelve tribes of Israel. He kept Jacob safe as he had promised in the dream at Bethel. He even made forward plans for keeping Jacob's family alive during the forthcoming famine.

>As Christians, we all make mistakes and we all find ourselves in places in life where we don't want to be. The wrong relationships, the wrong job, the wrong marriage – these things happen. Today, look back at your lowest point since you've been a Christian – but concentrate on where God has led you from there…

Airlock: Enthusiasm

Themes: **Justice, Irony, Conviction**

Watch out – God's about!

Decompress

'I say this because I know what I am planning for you,' says the Lord. 'I have good plans for you, not plans to hurt you. I will give you hope and a good future. Then you will call my name. You will come to me and pray to me, and I will listen to you. You will search for me. And when you search for me with all your heart, you will find me!' (Jeremiah 29:11-13)

NOW READ GENESIS 30:25-43

Immerse

Having struggled through 20 years of hard work for Evil Uncle Laban, God decides it's time to get his plan to make Jacob prosperous back on track again. There's a plot twist coming – a sudden change of direction and fortune. No, Laban is not suddenly punished by a plague of wives – his business starts losing value on the Mesopotamian Stock Exchange (North-Western Division).

>Laban tries to con Jacob out of his rightful wages by using his degree in Deception (First Class Honours), but he's forgotten the force of God. I'm pretty sure that waving a piece of bark at a sheep doesn't cause it to change colour (there's an experiment for some of you bored people to try!), but God blesses Jacob and the balance of power begins to shift...

>We're not sure exactly what is happening here, but there seems to be a bit of selective breeding going on. What the passage is clear about is that Jacob outwitted Laban and that God's plan would go from strength to strength.

Re-engage

God is a great comedian – he has a perfect sense of timing (being omniscient obviously puts him at an advantage here) and he is the absolute master of irony.

>Irony is all about justice – it's a bit like fate, but funnier. Irony demonstrates wrongness by showing justice, which is why it is so powerful and frequently humiliating and embarrassing. God uses irony a lot in the Bible. So be good. And watch out – God's about...

>There are times that we need to be taken down a peg or two – we've got things wrong but we haven't realised. Look back on how God has done this – both in 'convicting' you and in 'convicting' others. Is there anything you are being 'convicted' of now? Have a chat with God.

Airlock: Enthusiasm

Themes: **God's plan, Praise**

His father's son

Decompress

'Later, Jesus talked to the people again, saying, "I am the light of the world. The person who follows me will never live in darkness but will have the light that gives life"' (John 8:12).

NOW READ GENESIS 31:1–21

Immerse

Laban must have been furious to find that his game of hide-and-sheep had failed, and that Jacob's flock were breeding super-sheep whilst he ended up with lots of weak one… But suddenly comes one of the most important parts of God's plan – Jacob's moment of realisation – the 'a-ha' moment. He finally realises the significance of God's work in his life, and this is the first time we see the 'new Jacob', who really understands the God of his father and grandfather.

>There is a completely different atmosphere in this passage – notice how Leah and Rachel support their husband rather than squabbling over their differences. And notice how Jacob consults both wives as equals rather than ordering them to do as he says. Jacob's family are not over all their problems yet (the small matter of the Joseph saga – coming soon to a Bible reading guide near you), but they have got themselves to where God can work through them to complete this stage of the plan.

Re-engage

Of course, Jacob could have sat back and thought: 'Life is good! God is blessing me! I will soon be in charge of all of Laban's sheep. I'll stay here and die a very rich man.' And God would have been back to the drawing board again…

>It is easy to become comfort-blanket Christians, settled in work, church and social circles. But the time comes when that stage of the redemption plan is complete, and it's time to move on… or, in Laban's case, time to let go.

>Moving house or school, changing job, going to university – these are all difficult changes that we have to adjust to. But God has already planned exactly where you are going, and will make it clear through a variety of ways. (With me, he has to be obvious by turning down applications for the wrong university, failing interviews in the wrong city or having people coming up to me saying 'You really should work here' very loudly!)

>Don't be afraid if you have to move on – God does know what he's doing, even if you are taking a leap in the dark…

Airlock: Enthusiasm

Themes: **Anger, Confrontation**

Laban's 'A-ha' moment

Decompress

'From long ago, no one has ever heard of a God like you. No one has ever seen a God besides you, who helps the people who trust you.' (Isaiah 64:4)

NOW READ GENESIS 31:22–55

Immerse

There are some people who have a very short anger fuse – they get angry very quickly, explode like a small firework, shower someone with spit and then diffuse. There are other people – like me – who simmer with anger towards someone for zillions of years and then BANG! Bonfire night.

>Imagine having a fuse lasting 20 years – anger that has built up with every annoying, underhand thing that the other person has done. And what is worse, you can't really see the other point of view – you are in the right, the other person is clearly in the wrong.

>Did Jacob relish having to confront Laban? I doubt it. But unlike some of us, Jacob seems to be able to control his anger. It escapes as a low hiss, rather than exploding at his uncle. And it's far more effective! Jacob is not whining in the manner of a Moses or Jonah – he is speaking in the same clear and succinct tones as the later prophets. And this is how God can be sure he is ready for the next stage of the plan – the repopulation of Canaan.

Re-engage

You can always tell when God's working because the most unlikely people are touched when his plans are in action. In today's passage, it is Uncle Laban who sees something different in Jacob and is changed. Laban was touched enough to speak in the name of God by the end of the meeting.

>There are definitely times when God makes our friends and people around us more receptive to him by his intervention, and we need to pray that we'll have the right words to say at the right time.

>Think about the people who have influenced you since you became a Christian. Now (more tricky) think of those people that you have influenced since you became a Christian. Pray for both sets of people and yourself – you and they deserve it!

Airlock: Enthusiasm

My life plan:

_Start work
_7 years later…
_Get paid.
_7 years later…
_Get paid again.
_6 years later…
_Get paid, have it taken away, then get it back and move to new job.

God's plan for Jacob meant that he spent 20 years with an uncle that cheated him and treated him like a slave. What was the point of Jacob staying all that time in Mesepotamia? When you think about what God has in store for your life, would you be prepared to wait in a difficult situation for a long time?

Extra 1_ Genesis 12:1–9
Extra 2_ 1 Samuel 1:1–20

This is how they'll know

Themes: **Community**

Decompress

Father, help me be a strong member of your church, and a good advertisement for it.

NOW READ ACTS 9:32–43

Immerse

It seems to me that some churches spend so much time arguing that they don't get on with the serious business of telling people about Jesus. The worst thing about this is that it doesn't just confuse people on the outside (who often don't have a clue what we're arguing about), but it actually turns them away from Jesus. If we're supposed to be better, how come we're fighting? But look at the way the first Christians act in this story. Peter miraculously heals a sick man, and not only do people believe in Jesus on the strength of a miracle, but word gets around.

> Only a few miles away, a beloved member of the church falls ill and dies, and the Christians there immediately send for Peter, who they've heard is nearby. Peter comes, and prays for a miracle – and it's a miracle he gets.

> Would Peter have helped Tabitha out if she wasn't such a great person? Yes, he probably would. Whether he'd have heard about her getting ill at all is another question. Tabitha's love for her friends was reflected in their love for her. Jesus tells his disciples that this is how the world will know we're his followers: when we love each other (John 13:34,35). Acts of love, both among ourselves and to outsiders, not only bind us together – they communicate the love of Jesus in a way that's far more effective than words alone.

Re-engage

The members of the early church were in fear of their lives, and there's no denying that the constant danger encouraged them to stick together. It's easy to think that we're OK if we live in a country where Christianity is legal and kind of comfortable. We should be more thankful about the situation we're in, and not use it as an excuse to fight among ourselves. We might not see people raised from the dead quite as much as Peter did, but we can still look out for each other in the way that Tabitha did for the people in her church, and in the way they looked out for her. Maintaining an attitude of radical kindness towards each other brings us closer together, and brings all of us closer to God.

Airlock: Enthusiasm

Themes: **Change, Openness**

Get up and eat

Decompress

Lord, show me who I should be reaching out to. Give me the courage to talk about you to people I wouldn't usually speak to.

NOW READ ACTS 10:1–16

Immerse

Often I find myself watching films and TV programmes set in American high schools, and what always gets me is how they're so strictly divided into groups – the clever kids, the sporty kids, the nerdy kids, the alternative kids – which never have anything to do with each other. This is often reflected in the wider world.

> The laws of the Jewish religion forbade Peter from eating with non-Jews, and from eating loads of animals you wouldn't think twice about eating (and several you would – beats me why they bother telling the Jewish people not to eat bats, I wouldn't eat one). To go and eat 'unclean' food in an 'unclean' person's house was a really big deal. It meant Peter completely changing his way of life.

> There's no doubt that meeting Cornelius – and eating at his table – was what God wanted Peter to do, but Peter found it hard to take (v 14). It's quite likely that he agonised about it. But it was obvious that Cornelius believed and acted on his faith. The old rules kept him from hearing about Jesus, and so it was time for the old rules to be put aside. The good news was for everyone, and the old Jewish law was not going to get in the way. That's what the sheet full of animals signified.

Re-engage

We have to be aware of the traditions and rules that we follow, the way we talk, the way we behave. Do these things keep us from communicating with others? Try to be perceptive about what you do, and be honest about whether this keeps you from talking to people who are different to you. At the same time, be sensitive to other people's rules. Cornelius the Roman officer had already made the step of believing in God (rather than in the Roman gods) – Peter had to meet him halfway. Don't try to push your faith on people who aren't ready to hear it and put aside their own rules.

> Think about the people you know. Is there someone you wouldn't usually talk to? Find a way to talk to someone you wouldn't normally have anything to do with.

Airlock: Enthusiasm

Themes: **Change**

Turning point

Decompress

'Lord, help me to be aware of those times when a leap of faith is needed. Then give me the strength to take it.'

NOW READ ACTS 10:17–48

Immerse

Some people used to reckon that it was possible for a butterfly flapping its wings in Southern England to cause a hurricane in India. The tiny little disturbance of the air causes a slight breeze to change direction ever so slightly. This breeze affects a gust of wind. The gust of wind moves a larger amount of air and so on, until you get a hurricane. Dunno how scientific it is, but the same principle does work in human affairs. Revolutions begin with a word, a single action. Wars start with one shot (like the shot which killed the Archduke of Austria in 1914, eventually causing the First World War). The point is, one action can change things for good. Like dominoes, all sorts of things follow one by one, and the world is never the same again.

>Everything we do has consequences. God often uses what we do for him to change everything. Anything we do can be important, for good or bad. In today's passage, Peter knows that what he is doing is significant, but even he doesn't realise just how much of a difference sitting at dinner with this Roman soldier and his family will make. Peter wasn't ready for the ramifications of what he was doing. Later on, he even changed his mind for a while. But Peter knows that God wants him to do this – he's had a vision and Cornelius has met an angel.

Re-engage

With a few words about who Jesus is, Peter changes the course of history. The Holy Spirit falls upon the people at the meal and they all start speaking in different languages. Peter didn't have to follow God's guiding in this, and Cornelius didn't have to do what the angel said – they both could have dismissed what happened as a dream, and neither would have been any the wiser.

>Is God leading you to do something different and new? Remember that everything you do leads on to something, and that onto something else. Nothing you do for God is insignificant. Keep your eyes and ears open, and be ready to follow God's leading. Think and pray about the consequences of what you can do.

Airlock: Enthusiasm

Themes: **Change**

Ch-ch-ch-ch-changes

Decompress

'Father, help me, and the Christians around me, know when we need to accept change.'

NOW READ ACTS 11:1–18

Immerse

Change can be really scary. Leaving school and getting a job, or going to university; leaving home; meeting someone and deciding to get married – all of these things have the potential to alter the course of your life. Many people – and they're often decent, well-intentioned people – want to avoid change at all costs. It's not comfortable. You get this a lot in churches. In fact, it's churches that seem more prone to it than anywhere else.

>It doesn't have to be an important thing, either. We argue about every little change – from whether we should change to fair-trade coffee, to what colour the stair carpet in the church building should be, to whether we should sing a new song or not, to whether we should start up another Sunday service for all those people who aren't served by the ones we already have… Anything. And there's always a lovely honest decent Christian whose answer is, 'But we've always done it like this.'

Re-engage

Change is hard. But the early church rose to the occasion, and with a whole lot more at stake, as well. It's fairly easy to guess what the moral's going to be. When it's right to change – and by that, I mean change for God's sake, not for change's sake – we should not hesitate to change.

>Think about the things your church or youth group teaches. Think about the way they do things. What could change? Spend some time praying to God and asking whether there are changes that need to be made.

>All this talk about change is great, but where do we draw the line? What shouldn't we change?

Airlock: Enthusiasm

Themes: **Change, Mission**

Don't stop moving

Decompress

'Father, help me to keep on moving on, as you move in my life.'

NOW READ ACTS 11:19–30

Immerse

It's easy to think that once you've had a big upheaval and dealt with it, you're sorted, and you can just sit back and let things go. But a new start is just that – a new beginning, which implies there are going to be more things happening, and probably more changes along the way. A new beginning requires a new way of thinking.

>As I'm writing this, it's actually my wedding anniversary. When I think of how much I've changed in the way I live my life since the day we walked down the aisle, the mind boggles. I mean, hey, I even leave the seat down now. The point is, if I hadn't adapted to my circumstances, I'd probably be divorced now. A change of lifestyle – sharing a house with my wife – was one thing, but actually getting on with living together (and this goes for you too, darling) is another thing entirely.

Re-engage

Like the Christians in the passage, we have to not only adapt to both good and bad changes, but also make the very best out of them, using them as opportunities to tell people about Jesus and strengthen our relationships with each other, as well as with God.

>Think about the ways in which the world – and the church – is changing around you. Try to imagine how you'll deal with the future. Why not attempt to outline what you think church may be like in five, ten or more years into the future. How do you think it will have changed?

Airlock: Enthusiasm

Going to Cornelius' house took Peter way outside his comfort zone.

Are you happy in your own little world? Is God telling you to go somewhere where you might not feel so comfortable? If God asks you clearly to do something you don't feel comfortable doing, what will you say?

Extra 1_ Exodus 3:1 – 4:17
Extra 2_ Judges 6:11–40

Themes: **Faithfulness, Guidance**

Crazy in love

Decompress

'Even the foolishness of God is wiser than human wisdom, and the weakness of God is stronger than human strength'
(1 Corinthians 1:25).

>'The history of saints is mainly the history of insane people.'
(Benito Mussolini)

NOW READ PSALM 34

Immerse

Have you ever just gone up to someone in the street and told them God loved them? I'm guessing the person would probably think you were in some freaky brainwashing cult and therefore insane. Have you ever felt like God was giving you a wide open opportunity to tell someone, that very thing? The reaction can be quite different... Grown men breaking down in tears, women telling you they really needed to hear that today cos they felt that no one else did love them, people asking you to pray for them. That's the difference God's faithfulness can make, turning madness and randomness into the most perfect 'coincidences' in the world.

>We're told God works in mysterious ways, but if you trust what he's done in the past, and what he's going to do again in the future, then however random his instructions seem – either to you or the rest of the world – follow them. You know they're going to work out, cos God sticks to his promises.

Re-engage

Believing in God isn't always the most logical thing to do, and people can think we're crazy for it, but is that a bad thing? Are you 'insane' enough for people to notice? Are your beliefs and attitudes different to the crowd, and are you proud of them? Are you 'crazy in love' with God enough to trust the words of this psalm and believe in them?

>Are there any mad, crazy or even quite sensible things you feel God is calling you to do? Ask God to guide you, to show you what he wants you to do, or to open up the right doors for you to go through, keeping the wrong doors closed.

>Praying and reading the Bible is really important. Then, if you know, or you think you might know, go for it. It may be scary, but trust God's promises; sometimes you have to take a step of faith to continue walking the path set out for you. So start now, with prayer...

Airlock: Enthusiasm

Themes: **God's faithfulness, Faith**

That is sooo unfair!

Decompress

'Now faith is being sure of what we hope for and certain of what we do not see' (Hebrews 11:1, NIV).

NOW READ PSALM 35

Immerse

The idea of karma claims that what goes around comes around, so basically you get what you give and your good (or bad!) deeds will be revisted on you. Well, I wouldn't stake my life on it… A while back, some of my friends and I did some outreach work where we lived; a bit of social action, gardening for people, washing their cars etc. At the end of the week we had a barbecue and invited all the people in the community for a free burger. We got back after a really good night to find someone had broken into the house while we were out. My friend's bike and his PlayStation 2 had been stolen. Life's not fair, simple as.

>So who can you trust? Where's God in all this? Well, the thing about God's faithfulness is that we need to have faith in it in the first place. Reliability is all well and good when you can see what's going on, but what about when you can't? We found it hard to stand there and thank God for all the things he had done with that kind of an ending to the week. Can you trust in God's goodness when it's not right before your eyes?

Re-engage

Life is unfair to everyone, non-Christians and Christians alike, but with faith in God at least we have a hope to get us through the tough times. We know that God is always fair (v 24), always there for us (v 22), and always wants good for us (v 27). That's what faithfulness means: knowing that God is always good and can never be anything but good. Do you believe God when he says, 'I will save you'?

>In the hardest of times David managed to always tell of God's goodness and praise him every day. On my gap year we had to do a thing every morning called 'God is Top', where you had to think of a reason why 'God is Top' (or amazing, or even rock 'n' roll). It could be something specific he'd done the day before or just one of his characteristics or promises out of the Bible.

>Why don't you try doing this every morning, or whenever you see each other, to encourage each other and praise God for how great he is!

Airlock: Enthusiasm

Themes: **Faithfulness, Love, Evil**

A few of my favourite things

Decompress

'And so we know the love that God has for us, and we trust that love. God is love. Those who live in love live in God, and God lives in them' (1 John 4:16).

NOW READ PSALM 36

Immerse

Don't you just hate it when you're having the worst day ever and one of your really annoyingly happy friends comes up to you and says, 'Hey, at least you're alive!'

>'The truth is, I like this world. We've got dog racing, Manchester United... and we've got millions of people walking around like Happy Meals with legs.' (Spike, *Buffy the Vampire Slayer*)

>There's plenty of evil stuff in this world, but when big bad (albeit fictional) vampires can see the good there too, you realise things can't be all bad. Even the nastiest of criminals can love their mum, but sometimes you have to wonder where that little spark of goodness comes from...

Re-engage

There are a lot of things that God is in the Bible. He doesn't just love us, he is love, and he can never be anything but that. Everything about him is described to the max: his love can never be measured, it goes on for ever and ever. This psalm talks about him being light, or wisdom, and about his goodness and justice. Also, God made people in his own image (Genesis 1:27). We may have got a bit messed up, but can you still see the goodness in people like he can? Can you trust in God's unfailing love, despite the hatred and evil you see around you?

>Thank God for all the things you love about life.

>Thank you, God, that you gave us life in the first place, and thank you that you've filled it with so many good things. We're sorry we forget that we only have them because of you, especially when we let them get in the way of knowing you. Thank you that you sent Jesus to die for our sins so that we could know you. Please help us remember all this when we're surrounded by the bad things in the world that get us down. Amen.

Airlock: Enthusiasm

Themes: **God's faithfulness, Eternity**

Welcome to the diary room

Decompress

'We set our eyes not on what we see but on what we cannot see. What we see will last only a short time, but what we cannot see will last for ever' (2 Corinthians 4:18).

NOW READ PSALM 37

Immerse

What have those who trust the Lord, those who are not proud, those who are blessed by God and those who are good got in common? In Matthew 5:1–12, Jesus talks about similar groups of people inheriting the kingdom of heaven. All these people may have it rough here on earth, but God encourages them that in the end, they will be in a place where no evil can come against them, and God will comfort and honour them.

>As Christians, we know it isn't all about the here and now – we've got an eternity in heaven to look forward to. We trust in God's faithfulness to us because, even though we see people getting away with murder here, we know who's going to win in the final judgement. When everyone around you seems to be having fun doing things you know aren't right, be patient, and trust God when he tells you that you will get your rewards in heaven.

Re-engage

Verses 30 and 31 give us a pretty good model for surviving life here on earth. The good person manages to do what God wants them to do because they have read God's instructions and guidance. Romans 12 is a good place to start for practical advice. Read it, perhaps copy it out, but store it in your heart and live your life by it.

>What does verse 16 have to say about our current materialistic culture? How hard is it for you to be content with enough?

>How much are people motivated and led astray by money and possessions?

Airlock: Enthusiasm

Themes: **Faithfulness, Forgiveness**

Speak

Decompress

'God loved the world so much that he gave his one and only Son so that whoever believes in him may not be lost, but have eternal life' (John 3:16).

NOW READ PSALM 38

Immerse

Did you ever have memory verses to learn at Sunday school when you were little? I used to be the memory verse champion at my Sunday school. I had a terrible memory for everything else, but I could always remember what verse we had learned the previous Sunday!

>Memory verses have a tendency to stick in the mind like nothing else. When you feel so down that you haven't got any words to say to God, they pop up to remind you that 'Jesus loves you'. They are those little bits of the Bible which remind you that God is always good and always there for you, whatever the situation. You may not need them now, but it's always good to be prepared.

>Guilt and regret can really bog you down and make you feel like there's no way out; most of us have had times when we can sympathise with David's description. But don't stop calling out to God. He will always hear you, and he won't leave you – that's one of his promises (Deuteronomy 31:8). And possibly the most famous memory verse of them all (John 3:16) reminds us that there is a way out: we can have forgiveness and a new start because of Jesus Christ.

Re-engage

Is there anything you haven't let go of from your past? Most of the time it's harder for us to forgive ourselves than for God to forgive us and make it right again. David was humble before God; he knew he didn't have anything he could say to make it right (v 14). He confessed that he had done wrong and knew he deserved the punishment (v 18). But above all he trusted God (v 15).

>Trust that God does hear you, and will answer your prayers with the forgiveness he offers us through Jesus. Go and speak to him now.

Airlock: Enthusiasm

Life isn't fair, but do we get what we deserve, or would we even want to?

'Cheer up, love, it could be worse!' Imagine a world without any of God's goodness in it. What would it be like? What would you miss?

What memory verses do you know? Are there any key verses from the Bible which have helped you through tough times? If you don't know any memory verses, get learning!

Extra 1_ Romans 12
Extra 2_ Deuteronomy 6:1–9

Themes: **Courage, Embarrassment**

Ashamed of your faith?

Decompress

As you get dressed today, take a minute to think – would I be prepared to wear no clothes if God asked me to? Would I be prepared to be embarrassed for my faith? Ask God to give you courage to shine for him in any circumstance.

NOW READ ISAIAH 20

Immerse

When I was 13, I had a fantastic birthday party – all my friends, a sleepover, loads of food! Little did I know that this birthday would be one I would never forget or live down. About halfway through, the doorbell rang and in walked a bright yellow chicken – aka my dad. He cracked blown eggs on my friends' heads, and read out a poem he'd written about my old boyfriends, my hopes and fears, ending by saying he loved me and was sorry for being embarrassing.

>After being a social outcast for at least six weeks, I came to realise that, although it was the most humiliating thing that has ever happened to me (what will they do if I get married?!), it happened because my parents love me, and that is a strong commitment. My dad didn't mind being embarrassed; he was doing it for me because he loved me.

>I can't imagine walking around naked for three years like Isaiah did, but Isaiah had such a commitment to God that he was prepared to be humiliated for him. Through Isaiah's testimony, the Assyrian king defeated Egypt and Cush. Are you prepared to walk around naked if God asks you to? Are you ashamed of what you believe – or would you do the extraordinary for God?

Re-engage

It is against the law in most countries to walk around naked in public. It is not, however, against the law to step out in faith for God. Just as Isaiah trusted and obeyed God, we need to listen to God carefully and do what he says. Even if it seems a little odd, God does have a purpose and a plan for each of our lives, and he knows what's best. Are you ready and willing to do God's work?

>Think about ways you can show your friends and family that you are a Christian. Maybe you could start wearing a WWJD wristband and be prepared to talk about your faith as questions arise. The key to this is prayer (read Colossians 4:2). Ask God to be with you and to be your inspiration as you share your faith.

Airlock: Enthusiasm

Themes: **Waiting, Patience**

Are you ready for love?

Decompress

Waiting is funny, isn't it? Waiting for your birthday is great, but waiting to go into an exam is just plain nasty. God asks us to wait on him, so he can revive us and renew our strength. Pray that God will help you to be patient and wait for him to work out his plan for your life.

NOW READ ISAIAH 21

Immerse

Are you ready for what God has planned for you? Getting married isn't always a disaster, but it is something that you should be ready for and not rush into, unprepared. Here in chapter 21 Isaiah warns of a disaster coming, but the people are not ready for it. In Matthew 24:42 Jesus challenged his disciples about being ready and keeping a look out. He warned the disciples that God could come back to earth at any time and so we therefore need to be ready to answer him when he asks, 'Who do you think I am?' Is he the most important thing in your life?

>What would happen if Jesus came back today and asked you whether you believed in him? We need to be like the watchman in Isaiah who is committed to looking out, knows what to watch for and shares the good news. We need to be ready to answer Jesus when he asks his BIG question: who do you think I am?

Re-engage

Try to write down what you have done in your free time over the last week. Do you live your life to the full? If you knew that Jesus was returning to earth next week, what would you be doing differently? List the relationships you have at school, home, church, youth group etc. I have plenty of friends who I think I'll get round to telling about my faith eventually – but actually it's the most important thing. Are you ready?

Airlock: Enthusiasm

Themes: **Trust, Materialism**

Trust games

Decompress

Trusting somebody else can be hard. I can't stand that game where you fall backwards and the person behind you is supposed to catch you – I just bottle it every time! God, however, is never going to let you fall; we can always trust that he will be there. Pray today that you will learn to trust God with your whole life.

NOW READ ISAIAH 22:1–14

Immerse

Sometimes it's hard not to look for the most exciting place to be. Sometimes we just want to eat, drink and be merry. Sometimes it's hard to respect the past, when all you want to do is have fun now. In this passage the people of Jerusalem have lost the plot and forgotten who God is, what he has done in the past and what he could therefore do in the future.

>God has given us all the most amazing opportunity to know him through Jesus dying on the cross and rising again. We must not forget what God gave us – everything – and we should build our lives to reflect that. 1 Samuel 12:24 sums this up perfectly: 'You must honour the Lord and truly serve him with all your heart. Remember the wonderful things he did for you!'

Re-engage

Take a piece of paper, and draw a line along the bottom and a line on the left hand side. Label the line on the bottom, starting with the year you were born and ending with today's date. Think back over your life and write down what God has taught you throughout your life. You might want to mark a festival like Soul Survivor, or a Scripture Union holiday or mission that you attended. If you learnt a lot, put it up high; if something bad happened in your life, mark it as low – and then join up the dots. It's good to look back and realise that, in good and bad times, God speaks to us and provides for us. We can trust in him; that he has, is and will continue to look after us for ever.

Airlock: Enthusiasm

Themes: **Trust, Dependence**

The tooth fairy doesn't exist

Decompress

Trust can be a hard thing, especially when we trust people. Even our families let us down sometimes. Proverbs 3:5 says, 'Trust the Lord with all your heart, and don't depend on your own understanding.' Pray that God will give you the ability to trust him more than you trust the people you can see and touch.

NOW READ ISAIAH 22:15–25

Immerse

When I was little, I used to believe everything my parents told me, things like 'Father Christmas exists', 'The tooth fairy only visits people when they are sound asleep', and 'Liver tastes nice'. They also told me things about God, like 'God loves you', and, 'Jesus is the way to heaven'.

>Then, when I was about 10, a great aunt of mine died. I guess it was the first time I had thought about life being finite; that we all die. I started to question the very stuff of life and thought long and hard about faith. I realised that I needed to know Jesus as my friend and that it was a decision I needed to make. I couldn't rely on my parent's faith for my salvation. I needed to trust and believe in God myself rather than rely on Mum and Dad to get me to heaven.

>Relying on humans can seem far easier than trusting in God. We can see, touch and argue with humans, whereas God is a bit out of reach by comparison. In this passage Isaiah refers to Eliakim, describing him as trustworthy and dependable. The reality is that humans are not perfect; we muck up and do things that are not right. God, however, is always there; he does not use up all his compassion and then just sulk when we do things that aren't right. God is the only person you can fully trust and rely on.

Re-engage

Take some small squares of paper and draw or write on each one something from the past, present or future that you are fearful about, eg exams, boy/girlfriend, parents. Pray for one thing at a time and ask God to help you rely on and trust him with all of your concerns. In Philippians 4:6 it says, 'Do not worry about anything, but pray and ask God for everything you need, always giving thanks.'

Airlock: Enthusiasm

Themes: **Money, Materialism**

It's all about the bling, bling

Decompress

How much money do you get to spend a week – from a job, parents or other generous individuals? I reckon it's more than 50p. I would guess that you wouldn't think twice about spending 50p on something like a can of coke. There are some people in the world who have to survive on less than that a day. When I say survive, I mean that 50p has to buy food, light, somewhere to stay, clothes… everything. Do you take money for granted? Pray that God will show you how to be responsible with your money.

NOW READ ISAIAH 23

Immerse

Isaiah 23 tells the story of Tyre. It was a wealthy place by the sea which traded with many countries and had great influence. But the Lord (v 11) stretched out his hand and made the place tremble. Money and the power that comes from it can make anybody proud; too proud to wear a cheap watch, too proud to listen to God. Tyre fell from being a leader to being a refugee.

>Money and power are gifts from God that should never be taken for granted or misused. 1 Timothy 6:10,11 tells us that the love of money is the root of evil, and that instead we should try to follow God's path – a path of righteousness and faith in him, not in things that will fade away. Pray that God will show you how to remain faithful in all things, including your money and your lifestyle.

Re-engage

Open up your wallet or purse or piggy bank, and look at what's in there. Look around your room at all your possessions. Pray that God will show you how to use your things for his work. Think carefully about what you spend your money on and make sure that the way you think about money and the things you own show people that you love God.

>I knew a guy once who believed God wanted him to share everything he had. He used to let his neighbours borrow his car whenever they wanted, so much so that his neighbours went on holiday in his car, and his family went on the train. Pray that God will show you how to do good things with the gifts he has given you.

Airlock: Enthusiasm

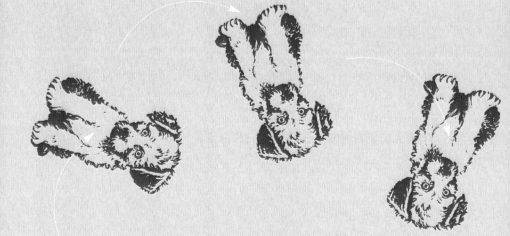

I've just run over your dog.
I don't like your cardigan.
Your boyfriend just snogged me.
Your new hair style makes you look like Marge Simpson.

What do you do when you have to say something to someone that you know they won't like. What kind of things might these be? Isaiah and the other prophets in the Bible often had things to say that the people would not have liked.

Are you ready to say something to someone that you know they won't like, but that you know you have to say? But how do you know that what you are going to say is right?

Extra 1 1 Kings 18,19
Extra 2 Matthew 3:1-12

Themes: **Heaven, Body image**

Ground force

Decompress

What do you think about heaven? Do you believe in it? What do you think it will be like? Who do you think will be there?

NOW READ 1 CORINTHIANS 15:35–49

Immerse

When you stop and think about it, seeds are amazing. The way that tiny specks of grit turn into big green and yellow flowery things later that year (aka plants), or the way a small round piece of polished 'wood' (aka a conker) grows into a huge tree producing its own playground weapons later that century. And to be honest, if we hadn't grown up being told about it in primary schools, we probably would never believe that something as small and dead looking as a seed could turn into something so big and alive, just with a bit of dirt, water and sunshine.

>Some seeds or nuts look cool (conkers), taste good (peanuts), or come in sweet packages (mangos), but if all we ever did was look at the seeds, eat them, or eat their 'wrappers', we'd miss out on their real potential.

>Paul says our bodies are like seeds which will die and be buried, but are just the start of something much bigger and better (which won't have all the bits we don't like now). And if he's right, we (and our world) might be in danger of looking at the seeds and never even thinking that they could 'grow' into anything else.

>If, like the people asking the questions Paul was writing about, we think that life after death is a crazy hope or an out of date superstition, we could be like the kid who's been given an X-box for Christmas, but only wants to play with the wrapping paper.

>Paul says that life now is just the start, and the best is still to come…

Re-engage

Look in a mirror. How do you feel about yourself and the body you have? Are you being harsher on yourself than anyone else ever would be? Have you believed the lie that you need to look like the digitally touched up, silicon filled, liposuctioned pictures of celebrities we see every day? Read 1 Corinthians 15:35–49 again, and when you look back into the mirror, remember that God did an amazing job making you, and that he's only just started…

Airlock: Enthusiasm

Eternity

Themes: **Death, Heaven**

Decompress

'Death, where is your victory? Where is your pain, place of death?' (1 Corinthians 15:55)

>Do you ever think about death? Does it make you feel victorious, or just scared?

NOW READ 1 CORINTHIANS 15:50–58

Immerse

Why are people scared of death? After all, it's one of the few things that's guaranteed in our lives is that one day we will die. Could it just be that most of us can't quite deal with the idea of being separated from the people who are part of our lives?

>But if Paul was right when he wrote 1 Corinthians 15, Jesus has taken away the stuff to be scared of. It doesn't mean that dying won't be painful, or that it's wrong to be sad when we miss someone who's died, but it does mean we can look at death differently.

>I don't often hear Christians talking about death or heaven. It might be because I live in a rich country where life isn't really that hard (for most of us anyway). In fact, to a lot of people who live around here, heaven doesn't sound great, because two holidays abroad each year, a car with air conditioning, more food than you could ever eat, home entertainment systems which make the cinema look low-tech, and cash in the bank is hard to beat. But in other parts of the world, where life is much closer to hell, heaven is something to look forward to.

>1 Corinthians 15 tells us that heaven has something you can't buy: the end of death. American scientists might be trying to make 'cryogenics' work, but nobody has so far managed to kill off death – apart from Jesus, who offers life that never wears out.

>When we get to heaven we will be made perfect. This perfection will last for ever, because there will be no death left to kill it off.

Re-engage

Look at your plans for the rest of today, or tomorrow. Are your plans something you'll be able to look back on from your seat in eternity and be proud of? The Bible might promise life for ever with God, but today (or tomorrow) will only come once – does that make you want to change your plans? Spend some time in prayer, discussing your plans with God.

Airlock: Enthusiasm

Themes: **Money, Giving**

8 Cashback?

Decompress

How do you feel about cash? Got enough? What do you do with it? What would you do with more?

NOW READ 1 CORINTHIANS 16:1-4

Immerse

Following Jesus isn't following instructions about money, but the way that practical stuff like cash (and giving it away) makes it into the final cut of the Bible means we can see it's important:

>It's about money for other people. Not for rich leaders, or even new church projects.

>The first day of the week (Sunday) was when Christians met to talk about and to God, and that's when they're told to give – as part of the way they worship God.

>Giving at the start of the week might tell us something about priorities too.

>Giving was supposed to be a regular part of life, not something to do when the celebrity leaders arrived. It doesn't just mean that it's less painful to give over a stretch of time. It probably means everyone gives more too.

>Paul didn't want everyone to give the same – he expected people to decide how much to give based on how much they were starting with, or 'put aside money as you have been blessed'.

>So, has much changed? Giving as part of our worship to God is the same. Making sure giving back to God is a priority is the same. Giving regularly is the same (even if electronic banking might mean there are easier ways of doing that now). Deciding how much to give based on how much we have to start with is the same.

>God doesn't have a cosmic calculator keeping tabs on how much we've given, but he does know how much we have, how much we need, how much it costs us to give, and what our giving says about how we feel about him. It's easy to think we'll wait until we're older or richer, but Jesus has major respect for the widow who gave a few pence, when it was all she had (Mark 12:41-44).

Re-engage

Stop and think about what God gives you in a week or month (not just cash, but other things which keep your life running). How much of it do you pass on to other people, as giving back to God? Does that giving match with how much you say you love God (we should only give what is ours to give – don't get into debt by giving the bank's money away)?

Airlock: Enthusiasm

Themes: **Time, Relationships**

The louder you scream...

Decompress

'The louder you scream, the faster we go.' How fast does your life feel? So slow you wonder if it's going anywhere, or so fast you never really get chance to see what's going on around you?

NOW READ 1 CORINTHIANS 16:5-9

Immerse

We must cram more into our lives than any group of people ever has before us. People are living longer than anyone can remember. And technology means we can fit more into a day than at any other time in history. The average American family spent 30 hours a week on housework in 1965 compared to 1995's 17.5 hours a week. You can see how much time is freed up for enjoying life (or fitting more in). And that's without thinking about the communication or transport revolution (who would ever have believed that we could send files and pictures to the other side of the world instantly?).

>When 1 Corinthians was written, everything took a whole lot longer. Planning to take a trip from Ephesus to Corinth (just a couple of hundred miles across the Mediterranean – which we could do on a plane in less than an hour) was a major deal. You didn't go for a day. You could end up going for a whole winter.

>Technology's great – I'd be stuffed without it, and if someone could give me a choice between life in the first or 21st century AD, I'd go for the 21st every time. But in our world where we talk about people having 'quality time' together (to cover over the fact that we hardly ever get time to talk), do you ever think there are some things we could learn from 1 Corinthians' low-tech world?

Re-engage

Relationships take time – going out with someone, being a friend, being a son/daughter, working with people, trying to introduce people to Jesus, helping new followers of Jesus work out their new lives – there's no shortcut to getting to know people. You have to spend time with them.

>Now life runs at a different speed, are we giving people enough time? Is our timetable God's, or have we got it so planned out that God has to try and keep up with us?

Airlock: Enthusiasm

Themes: **Leaders, Good examples**

Faith academy

Decompress

'Look deep into my heart, God,
and find out everything I am
thinking.
Don't let me follow evil ways,
but lead me in the way that time
has proved true.'
Psalm 139:23,24 (CEV)

NOW READ 1 CORINTHIANS 16:10-24

Immerse

Reading the end of these New Testament letters can seem a bit boring, but when you take another look, there is more to this stuff than just a list of names.

>Timothy (vs 10,11) – a leader in the first group of Christians. Paul spent time building him up (1 Timothy 4:11,12), and getting him support with other Christians, even though he was young.

>Apollos (v 12) – like Paul, a bit of a celebrity in the New Testament churches. We know (1 Corinthians 1:12) some people set up Paul, Apollos and a couple of other 'celebrity leaders' as rivals. But Paul doesn't see them as competition. He's interested in God's work being done – not who does it.

>Alert. Strong. Courage. Love. (vs 13,14) – because this is in the last few sentences of the letter, it must be important stuff; the Big Picture kind of stuff people say to each other if they're not going to talk for a while.

>Stephanus, Fortunatus and Achaicus (vs 15–18) – we don't know much about these guys, but Paul had respect for them, their history, and their work. He thought it was important that the members of the church in Corinth gave them respect too.

>Aquila and Priscilla (v 19) – a married couple who we hear about in other bits of the New Testament. In a sexist culture which didn't let women have much profile or respect, the first Christians, like Jesus, were way ahead of their time, and gave women like Priscilla respect and responsibility.

Re-engage

If we were in the Faith Academy, how would we do as Christians with our lives under the microscope (make that cameras) 24/7?

>Think about who your 'leaders' are, or should be. Are you ready to respect, listen to, and follow them? Think about who looks up to you as a leader. Could they write some of this stuff about you, telling people to follow your example?

>Spend some time talking to God in prayer about your leaders and your role.

Airlock: Enthusiasm

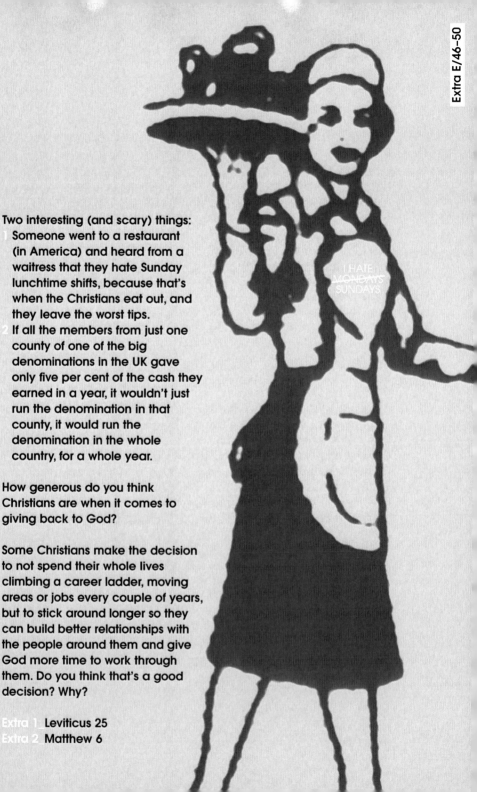

Two interesting (and scary) things:
1. Someone went to a restaurant (in America) and heard from a waitress that they hate Sunday lunchtime shifts, because that's when the Christians eat out, and they leave the worst tips.
2. If all the members from just one county of one of the big denominations in the UK gave only five per cent of the cash they earned in a year, it wouldn't just run the denomination in that county, it would run the denomination in the whole country, for a whole year.

How generous do you think Christians are when it comes to giving back to God?

Some Christians make the decision to not spend their whole lives climbing a career ladder, moving areas or jobs every couple of years, but to stick around longer so they can build better relationships with the people around them and give God more time to work through them. Do you think that's a good decision? Why?

Extra 1 Leviticus 25
Extra 2 Matthew 6

Themes: **Obedience, Repentance**

How to calm a storm

Decompress

Our narrator takes a seat by the fireside and starts to tell us a short story – the story of Jonah. Our narrator knows that God is King over all the world. You cannot flee from him. His tale is for any who think they know better. It is a tale about a prophet, a real prophet named in the Bible's history books.

NOW READ JONAH 1

Immerse

So who was Jonah? Well he gets a mention in one of the Bible's historical books. Check out 2 Kings 14:25. Same guy. This book was written a couple of centuries after his death so the story may be history or may be legend. It makes little difference to the lessons.

>What of Nineveh? It was the capital of Assyria – not a Jewish city. It is likely that Jonah's natural reaction to God's call was to disbelieve it; his preference would have been for Nineveh to be destroyed. It was the capital city of Israel's historical enemy, and one of its cruellest enemies too. Huddesfield, Chester, Ipswich, Telford and Nuneaton had populations of around 120,000 according to the 1991 census, roughly the same size as Nineveh was in Jonah's day.

Re-engage

The narrator of Jonah strikes the high-water mark of practical Old Testament theology. Nothing else in the Jewish scriptures sets forth more clearly the character of God, his love for all people and his willingness to forgive the most sinful of people.

>Jonah found himself with nothing. No property. No friends. No lifebelt. No hope. Take a moment to take stock and list the things you would miss if you were 'thrown overboard'. Now list the things that would be useful to have with you. All Jonah had with him was a rather tattered relationship with his creator.

>A prayer: 'God help me to be obedient before it's too late.'

Airlock: Enthusiasm

Themes: **Prayer, obedience**

Tips from the swallowed

Decompress

You hear people say, 'If only I had the time and the space I would pray more.' Do you think being swallowed by a whale is what they have in mind?

NOW READ JONAH 2

Immerse

Have you ever listened to the story of a survivor? People who have been rescued from certain death value life more highly than most.

>The movie *Unbreakable* deals with such a theme. David Dunn, played by Bruce Willis, is a man who is the only survivor of a horrific train crash. Everyone else has been killed and Dunn is unscathed. Why? The film deals with his quest to find out his mission in life and if he is truly 'unbreakable'.

>Jonah's sea-trip, ending with him becoming living fish-puke, ensures he will face his God with rapt attention next time. Chapter 2 interrupts the story. The writing stops being narrative and becomes psalm-like. In fact, much of what Jonah prays is from the psalms. It has all the hallmarks of a 'last resort' prayer, right down to the promise to turn to God if he gets him out of this mess. It is remarkable eloquence on the lips of someone who is being digested.

>It's a fascinating prayer. It wavers between hopeless despair (in verses 3,4,5 and 6) and the assumption that God is already on the case (in verses 2,4 and 6).

Re-engage

In the belly of the fish Jonah had nothing. What would you pray for if you had nothing? Do you thank God for all the things you normally take for granted, as Jonah did? When do you spend most time in prayer – when things are great or when things are bad?

>Wherever you are, whatever your circumstances, pray your own words. Tell God what you think of him, mixing praise and despair if you want to. When is a good time to pray? Now.

Airlock: Enthusiasm

Themes: **Repentance**

Second chance

Decompress

Sometimes, when we mess up, we get another opportunity to do it right. Do you take the second chances you get?

NOW READ JONAH 3

Immerse

I was a stubborn child. Whenever I got told off, but then got the chance to do things properly, I wouldn't. I would sit there in a battle of wills with my parents, determined not to do it out of principle. What my principles were, I'm not sure, but I was sticking to them. It was stupid, of course, but I was too proud to give in.

>When his second chance came around, however, Jonah went straight to Ninevah to deliver God's message. He has learnt a lot, it seems, about God's plan and that God really does know what he's doing.

>But what surprises me about this passage (and I think it surprises Jonah too) is the speed with which the king and people of Ninevah respond to Jonah's message. It seems almost instantaneous, with everyone in the city joining in with the repentance.

>This is probably one of the most surprising and miraculous conversions in the Bible. Jonah's short message of God's judgement causes the whole city to repent. One of the most evil and pagan cities in the world stops being nasty and says sorry. Ninevah grabs its second chance with both hands (if a city can have hands...).

Re-engage

Is there someone you know to whom you should be giving a second chance? It's easy to want to stay angry with someone who has hurt you, but the story of Ninevah shows us that God delights in making things right, in giving people second chances. He does not hold grudges against people.

>Shouldn't we follow his example? If God's message can turn a whole city, then surely acting in a way that shows God's love can start the healing process. God made the first move with the people of Ninevah, so why don't you make the first move?

Airlock: Enthusiasm

Theme: **Mercy, Love**

How to irritate God

Decompress

'It's not fair.' How many times have you said that since the age of 3? Lots, probably.

NOW READ JONAH 4

Immerse

Who on earth said life should be fair? On being given a parking ticket by a police officer, so many people respond by suggesting the police are wasting time and should be dealing with 'real' criminals.

>Jonah is upset and angry. 'Told you so,' he says. 'I knew you'd do that.' And he tells us why he ran away in the first place: '…you are … slow to anger and abiding in love…' (v 2) – unlike Jonah.

>'My people like killing our enemies, not loving them,' says Jonah. 'How dare you have mercy?' Jonah was pleased when God saved him from certain death, but upset when God saved the people of Nineveh.

>So he sits down (4:5) and a nice plant appears to give him shade. Then God destroys Jonah's shady plant just when he was enjoying it.

>Jonah begrudges God's mercy to the heathen, yet gets angry when he shows no mercy to a plant. Gods uses the plant to make his point. Jonah is a disappointing prophet and God, the real hero of the story, achieves his purposes despite Jonah, not because of him.

>Jonah asks God to end his life (4:3,9). Haven't we been here before? (1:12)

Re-engage

Cracking story; rubbish prophet. We've had a fish with a sense of direction, mass repentance following a short message, and a king going round in goat-hair knickers and covering himself in ashes. Meanwhile Jonah cries over the death of a plant but is not happy at the survival of a city.

>The book of Jonah is a handbook on how not to be a prophet. It says to us, 'Do you really believe that God loves everyone equally?'

>Thankfully there are characters in the Bible who didn't get everything right. Pray that you can be obedient. Pray for God to have mercy on people who don't seem to deserve it.

Airlock: Enthusiasm

Themes: **History**

Jonah: did it happen?

Decompress

Some of the Bible is history. Some is story. The whole of it is his story.

NOW READ JONAH 1–4 AGAIN (GO ON, IT'S A GOOD STORY)

Immerse

People have argued about whether the story of Jonah is historical or not. I mean, we're talking big fish and the whole of a very nasty city simply saying sorry! Let's have a quick look at the 'So did it really happen?' problem. Here's what some experts say:

> 'Quite obviously, it ... should not be read as an historical event.' (Gerhard Von Rad, *Old Testament Theology Volume 2*, Oliver and B, 1962)

> 'This is not a biographical account of what actually happened in the experience of the prophet ... but a short story told to drive home a prophetic message to the writer's generation.' (Bernhard W Anderson, *The Living World of the Old Testament*, Longman, 1988)

> 'The attempt to interpret the book as a straightforward historical report met with resistance at a very early date.' (Brevard S Childs, *Introduction to the Old Testament as Scripture*, SCM, 1979)

> 'The popular modern view is that Jonah was written as an imaginative tale ... but there is no positive evidence ... to show that...' (*The New Bible Commentary: Revised*, Inter-Varsity Press, 1970)

> To summarise: a survey of conservative scholarship reveals that only the most conservative of conservatives would treat this as history. But what do you think? And why? Does it matter whether the story is real or not? What is the book really saying to us?

Re-engage

Jonah's message in Jonah 3:4 is seven words long – an effective short piece of communication. Sometimes the right word, in the right place, at the right time, is better than any fancy speech. God's word is always effective (Hebrews 3:12,13).

> Today, give someone a second chance. Write letters to MPs, local councils or world leaders about situations that you think should be changed.

Airlock: Enthusiasm

JONAH!

The Bible is full of accounts of things you wouldn't expect holy people to do:

Use sarcasm and encourage violence (Elijah)
Marry prostitutes (Hosea)
Cook on dung (Ezekiel)
Eat locusts (John the Baptist)

But all of them are things God told them to do. Jonah doesn't work like that. This prophet is like no other biblical prophet. Jonah did everything he could not to do what God asked.

Is God asking you to do something?
Is it something you want to do?
Are you going to do it?

Extra 1 Hosea 1,3
Extra 2 Matthew 21:28–32

Themes: **Miracles, Taxes, Authority**

Financial fixes 'n' fish fingers

Decompress

What's the best surprise you've ever had? Do you remember how you felt? What were your feelings towards the surprise-giver?

>When was the last time you were surprised by God?

NOW READ MATTHEW 17:24–27

Immerse

The other week I bought a packet of fish fingers. I took them home and prayed over them, raising my hands and doing some very godly shouting as the fishy treats defrosted on our kitchen table. After much fevered godliness and spiritualness, I opened the box… Lo! The exact amount for the council tax was between the golden crumbs!

>Errr… you may have spotted that that wasn't quite true. Financial need plus seafood does not equal instant cash. It would be great if we could find money in the freezer cabinet, but that doesn't seem to happen very often.

>On the other hand, my mobile broke last month and I couldn't afford a new one. I was gutted and prayed about it and I got sent an anonymous Carphone Warehouse voucher through the post. I couldn't have been more gobsmacked if it had arrived in a mackerel.

>Whenever Jesus interacts with someone, it's always fascinating and he always shows more of his character. Look again at this passage and the conversation between the two friends. If this passage was all we knew about Jesus, what could we say about him?

>The real issue is not how Jesus got his tax, but why he paid it. Whether Jesus agreed with paying taxes or not wasn't the issue. He didn't even think it was worth having a big debate about. The most important thing was how other people were going to feel and react. Having talked through the issue with Peter, he decided that the principle was far less important than the repercussions.

Re-engage

Looking at verse 27, what does that mean for us? How should we react to traditions? Or strange laws?!

>Lots of us find it hard to obey authority. If a rule doesn't make sense, we kick against it automatically. You may not get the chance today, but at some point this week try to practice 'obedience' (this is especially tough with parents!) – not without question, but without attitude.

Airlock: Enthusiasm

Themes: **Temptation**

Eyeball transplants

Decompress
What sins do you really struggle with? Not the ones that are OK to talk about with your friends, but the ones that only you and God know about. Talk with God about them now and leave the problem with him. Even if it's for the hundredth time…

NOW READ MATTHEW 18:1–9

Immerse
I can't stop thinking about that bit in *Minority Report* where Tom Cruise decides to endure an eye transplant to avoid having his retinas scanned by the pre-crime machines. It's a pretty gross concept and seeing his old eyeballs waved around in a little sandwich bag afterwards is an image that's stayed with me! But, his eyes were causing him problems so he decided to remove them – isn't that what Jesus is saying?!

>Tom was pretty lucky in that he got a new pair of non-problem eyes. Unfortunately, I'd probably end up like the Philosopher's Axe. There's this story about a Philosopher who has an axe (so far, so easy!), but the handle conks out so he replaces it. Then the head gets all dull and rusty so he replaces that too. His dilemma is this – is it the same axe? If I could replace all the bits that cause me trouble I'd end up like 'The Philosopher's *Airlock* Writer' – new eyes, new hands, new feet, new heart, new brain…

Re-engage
The main problem for me is that the 'bits' that cause us to sin most often aren't really optional extras: heart and brains and err… essential bits. Even if we did remove our arms, our eyes and our tongues, we'd still be thinking the same thoughts, just not acting on them!

>What else could 'cut it off and throw it away' mean? One possibility is to cut yourself off from a situation. Next time you think you're just going to completely lose it with your brother or sister because they're an annoying brat, try getting out of the room. Distance may not always be the answer but it can be a good short-term solution if you're feeling weak and just can't resist the temptation!

>I love the phrase 'flee from sin!'. There are so many times I should have just legged it! Maybe it's time to cut yourself off from a temptation. Please though, don't get any knives out and start chopping! Especially when it comes to siblings.

Airlock: Enthusiasm

Themes: **Love, Evangelism**

Rah-Rah-Rasputin

Decompress

'I am the good shepherd. I know my sheep, as the Father knows me. And my sheep know me, as I know the Father. I give my life for the sheep.' (John 10:14,15)

>The shepherd knows you. Just think about that.

NOW READ MATTHEW 18:10–14

Immerse

Rasputin is a pretty famous figure in Russian history for being very friendly with the Tsarina and miraculously surviving being poisoned, shot and drowned (well, he did die eventually, but he staggered about for a long time first). He's also notorious for holding the view that to be really close to God you've got to sin a lot, the dirtier the better, because if you've sinned lots you need to be forgiven a lot and so you love God more.

>He was basically saying, if God really loves the lost sheep more than all the others, we should go and get lost. Logical! And tempting? If you've ever tried it yourself, you'll know that it's not much fun. Getting lost means falling down cliffs, getting stuck in thorny hedges, being really cold and not having enough to eat. OK, so that's all analogy but you can translate it pretty easily into your life. Most of all though, it means the shepherd's got to follow you through it all with his heart aching to find you.

Re-engage

Verse 12 shows how God values every individual. It's easy to lose that perspective ourselves. How should God's attitude shape how we treat the 'lost sheep' around us? And if we're a bit lost ourselves, how should it affect how we see the person in the mirror?

>Get yourself a little Shaun the Sheep (one of those *Wallace and Gromit* ones) and stick it next to your PC. Every time you look it in the eye, send up a prayer for a person you know who needs to come back into God's arms. And if you feel that's you, Shaun can remind you that God's out there looking for you.

Airlock: Enthusiasm

Themes: **Tough love, Prayer**

Hug those with bad breath

Decompress

Sometimes loving people can be at a high price to yourself, especially when you're saying things they don't want to hear. Is there anyone around you who needs 'tough love'? Lift them up to God.

NOW READ MATTHEW 18:15–20

Immerse

Someone close to me is an alcoholic. I'll call them Monty as it's a great name and makes me think of dead parrots. A mutual friend tried to discuss the problem with Monty and got laughed at. After a bit of discussion, a couple of family members went to broach the subject and got shouted out of the house. Perhaps, if we were Americans, we would have had an 'intervention' (where the whole family group and a bunch of friends would get together and force Monty to recognise his problem), but instead we felt we had to give up.

>Jesus seems to be suggesting a similar approach with people who get caught up in doing the wrong thing, minus the 'giving up' part. You go and see the person, then if that doesn't work, get some (loving!) back-up. And if that still fails, perhaps the shock tactic of a large group of like-minded people will help the person. It's only then that Jesus changes tack and suggests treating them as 'tax collectors'.

>But remember how Jesus treated tax collectors?

Re-engage

When someone does something wrong, our initial reaction is often to pull away from them, sometimes out of revulsion and sometimes out of self-protection. Jesus' world is an upside-down one in that he encourages us to get close to the people we dislike, and embrace those who repulse us.

>Is verse 15 too idealistic to actually act on? If someone in your church really hurts your feelings or treats you badly, do you think you could go up to them and tell them so (in a LOVING way!)? With Jesus' help this should be a reality for us. We should be able to address personality clashes and arguments by bringing them out into the open. Is there anyone who you're really struggling with at church? Could you prayerfully address that problem directly with them rather than talking about them behind their back or bottling it up, getting more and more resentful?

Airlock: Enthusiasm

An eye, a tooth...

Decompress

'I'll only forgive her if she NEVER does it again!'
'I'll only forgive him if he says he's sorry and really means it!'
   >Is it possible to forgive with no strings attached?

NOW READ MATTHEW 18:21–35

Immerse

Your brother steals your CDs for the eighth time this week and he's sat on two of them so the cases are cracked. According to the passage, how should you respond?
   >The people at church totally ignore what you've got to say and don't understand what you need to get close to God. How would Jesus expect you to respond?
   >There's no Dr Pepper left AGAIN, even though everyone knows you don't like the other stuff. What does verse 22 suggest you should do?
   >Your best friend is now going out with the person you TOLD them you were interested in. They're so selfish. From this part of Matthew, what should your reaction be?
   >You've been abandoned, hurt and left to feel worthless. According to the passage, how should you respond?
   >I'm sorry the questions are repetitive, but it's so hard to grasp – there aren't any exceptions.

Re-engage

Verse 35 shows how seriously God takes us not forgiving each other; he's made it the sole condition of forgiving us. If you feel resentment, anger or hurt towards someone, take the first steps towards forgiving them by telling God how you feel. Forgiving this person may be an ongoing process. Writing down what this person has done can help to get the emotions out. Give it over to God and then destroy the paper.
   >You may have to do it all over again tomorrow, but you've forgiven them today.
   >NB God is, of course, incredibly angry when anybody hurts us. If you have ever been badly hurt (perhaps because of abuse or attack), forgiveness may not even be on your agenda – you're just coping. Whatever you do, don't feel guilty about this but go and talk to somebody you trust – preferably an older Christian whose advice you can rely on.

Airlock: Enthusiasm

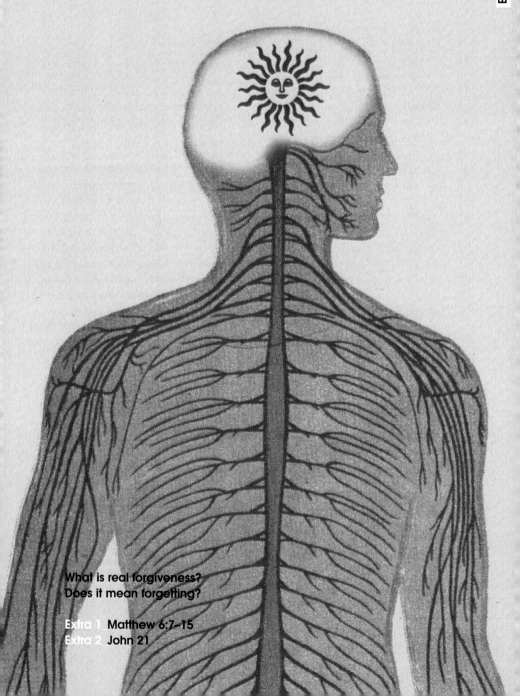

Themes: **Trusting God, Prayer**

Wake up!

Decompress

'Wake up, sleeper!
Rise from death,
and Christ will shine on you.'
(Ephesians 5:14)

NOW READ ACTS 12:1-19

Immerse

How often is this true of us? (Not the being woken up in prison by an angel bit.) We pray and pray for something to happen, desperate for God to help us – but are we still surprised when he does?

>Peter trusted God with his life to such an extent that he was able to sleep peacefully in a prison cell, awaiting his death. But even with such a strong faith in God, he was still astounded by the miraculous way that God rescued him.

>The other believers, Peter's friends, were desperately worried about Peter, as well as being concerned for their own safety. So they met together and prayed through the night, asking God to save him. They prayed because they believed that God was powerful and could perform impossible miracles. But when the miracle they had prayed for occurred, they couldn't believe it was true.

>Even when our faith in God is strong, even when we've witnessed miracles in our own lives, it's still hard to get our heads around the true awesomeness of God.

Re-engage

What impossible situation have you been praying about? Do you really believe that God can sort it out? Ask him to expand your vision of what he is truly capable of.

>Have you ever prayed for something miraculous to happen, and then tried to explain it away as a coincidence when it did happen? Why doesn't God always intervene miraculously in all our difficult situations?

Airlock: Enthusiasm

Themes: **Punishment, God's plan**

Death by worms

Decompress

'Love the Lord, all you who belong to him.
The Lord protects those who truly believe,
but he punishes the proud as much as they have sinned.'
(Psalm 31:23)

NOW READ ACTS 12:19B–25

Immerse

This is a strange passage. It seems to be saying that if you don't give God the glory, he'll smite you down and you'll be eaten to death by worms. Not a pleasant thought. But perhaps we need to look at the big picture here.

>Herod was a corrupt king who hated Christians and was trying to stop God's message from spreading. Although God isn't malicious, he is just. And justice means that sin has to be punished. Fortunately, for you and me, Jesus took the punishment for all our sins when he died on the cross, so we don't have to worry about getting attacked by any killer worms. But Herod refused to accept that God deserved all the glory – he wanted to keep some for himself, and so it was his pride that led to his death.

Re-engage

When things go wrong in our lives, we're always quick to ask God, 'Why?', or to beg for his help. But what about when things go right? When we've passed a difficult exam, been promoted at work or received recognition for a sporting achievement, do we remember to give the glory to God, or do we keep it for ourselves?

>Make a list of the good things in your life – your successes, the things you're proud of. They don't have to be big things – you might be pleased with yourself for not shouting at your sister today, or for remembering to hand in your homework.

>Now try to imagine how you would have achieved those things without God. Would it have been harder? Would any of them have been impossible? Now thank God for each one, and ask him to help you put him first in every area of your life.

Airlock: Enthusiasm

Themes: **God's plan, Mission**

Your mission...

Decompress

'Then I heard the Lord's voice, saying, "Whom can I send? Who will go for us?"
So I said, "Here I am. Send me!"'
Isaiah 6:8

NOW READ ACTS 13:1–3

Immerse

So, in *The Fellowship of the Ring*, the Council of Elrond are all arguing about who should take the ring to be destroyed in the fires of Mount Doom, and suddenly a little voice cuts through the din, saying, 'I will take the ring to Mordor ... though I do not know the way.'

>Being chosen for a special task can be an immensely proud moment, but it can also be terrifying. And even though the choice is usually made by someone else, there is still that moment when you have to decide to take up the challenge, or to refuse it.

>As the leading members of the church pray and fast, the Holy Spirit singles out Saul and Barnabus for a special task. They are then prayed for, and sent out on their first missionary journey to spread the good news about Jesus. A big challenge; a big responsibility. But Saul and Barnabas know that God has chosen them for this task, and will be with them as they take it on.

Re-engage

We're not all chosen by God to go out on high-profile missionary assignments like this one, but God does have a special purpose for each of our lives. He may have chosen you to go out to tell thousands of people about Jesus; or he may have chosen you to practically demonstrate Jesus' love to the thousands of people who buy their cheese from you at Sainsbury's. Whatever you are doing, you can choose to do it for God, or you can choose to ignore him. God has chosen you, but you have to make the decision to follow him.

>Spend some time thinking about how God is working in your life at the moment. Are you helping to lead people in worship by playing your drums at church? Are you living out your faith at school by being a good friend? Whatever your situation, God can use you to do something special, perhaps something that only you can do. Ask him to show you how.

Airlock: Enthusiasm

Theme: **Power, Evangelism**

In the dark

Decompress

'The Light shines in the darkness, and the darkness has not overpowered it.'
(John 1:5)

NOW READ ACTS 13:4–12

Immerse

I knew a girl at school, let's call her Lindsey, who was quite interested in hearing about God, and often asked me about what I did at church – but only when no one else was around. If her best friend, Angela, overheard us talking, she would come over and start making fun of me and what I believed, and Lindsey would take her side and laugh along with her. It was really frustrating because I knew Lindsey really wanted to know about God, but she was just too scared to stand up to Angela – she didn't want to risk her friendship or her reputation.

>Paul and Barnabus came up against a similar problem in Cyprus. The governor, Sergius Paulus, wanted to hear the message of God, and invited them to visit him. But his sidekick, a dodgy magician called Elymas, didn't want Sergius to hear about God – he was probably afraid that Sergius would realise that he was a fraud, and get rid of him. So Elymas did his best to stop Sergius from believing Paul's message. But Elymas had underestimated the power of the Holy Spirit who was working through Paul, and he was the one who ended up being well and truly left in the dark.

Re-engage

Unfortunately, God doesn't often zap people with temporary blindness when they try to stop us telling people about him. (Although it could be quite fun if he did…) The important thing is to recognise when something, or someone, is blinding people to God's message, and to ask God to show you how to deal with it.

>Ask God to help you with the gift of discernment. This basically means that God will help you see when something is up, and you will be able to tell what it is – and with God's help you may be able to sort it out.

Airlock: Enthusiasm

Themes: **Including everyone**

Are you on the guest list?

Decompress

'...The king said to his servants, "The wedding feast is ready. I invited those people, but they were not worthy to come. So go to the street corners and invite everyone you find to come to my feast." So the servants went into the streets and gathered all the people they could find, both good and bad. And the wedding hall was filled with guests.'
(Matthew 22:8–10)

NOW READ ACTS 13:13–52

Immerse

>Paul and Barnabas have some great news, and they want to share it with their own people, the Jews. So they go and preach in the synagogue, they lay out all the evidence, backing up their arguments with Old Testament scriptures. But the Jews aren't interested. Only a few of them accept the truth. The people who do listen and believe are the non-Jews, the foreigners – the people who had previously been excluded from 'God's chosen people'. But when they start following Jesus, the Jews get a bit annoyed…

Re-engage

So what does this have to do with us? What can we learn from it? Well, basically, this passage is one of the many in the New Testament that shows us Jesus' party isn't exclusive – everyone is invited, and it's free for all. But you do need to be in it to win it. You need to get your name on the guest list. You need to accept his invitation. Even if your friends aren't interested and the only people you know that are going are a bit nerdy and uncool. Cos if you turn down the invitation now, you can't complain later when you're stuck on the outside watching everyone else having a good time.

>Next time you walk through the playground at school, or sit in the common room, or meet some friends for a drink, look out for anybody who might be feeling excluded – either from your group of friends, or from society in general. Remember that Jesus wants them at his party too (yes, even the smelly boy with greasy hair who always sits in the corner and never changes his clothes), but they might need you to invite them. Think of a way to include them this week.

Airlock: Enthusiasm

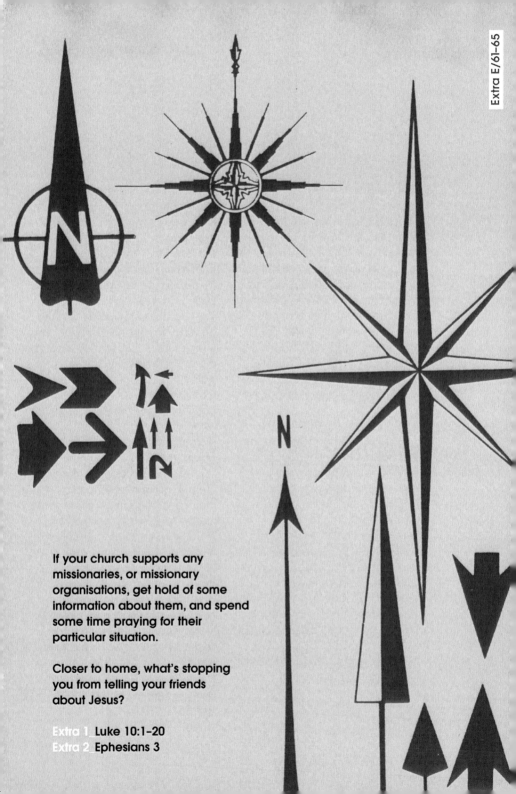

If your church supports any missionaries, or missionary organisations, get hold of some information about them, and spend some time praying for their particular situation.

Closer to home, what's stopping you from telling your friends about Jesus?

Extra 1 Luke 10:1-20
Extra 2 Ephesians 3